"REALLY enjoyed it! It put words to the frustrations I have been feeling with the political realm and how it has infiltrated Christianity in so many ways. The historical development of how that all happened was very interesting and enlightening."

Inga Johnson
Long time faithful friend and parishioner

"As much as the stats bemoan losing the Millennial generation, Tri brings hope that the future is not lost on them but rather we are in a time of preparation for a spiritual awakening in the Church in the West. He courageously and boldly describes what that awakening might look like and how an authentic faith of following the way of Jesus will lead to many encountering the transforming love of the Father, Son and Holy Spirit. I believe that Tri as pastor, missiologist and prophet has given us a path for prayer and repentance. Prayer for the Spirit of God to open hearts to the Good News and repentance, hearing the Spirit and turning our hearts to align with what God is doing in our day and our time. I heartily commend to you Re:Form without apology. Tri Robinson brings clarity to the cluster of issues around the future, the hope of the gospel in our day and in our time."

Rose Madrid Swetman, D.Min
Vineyard NW Regional Leader

This is a great book which ends too soon. And just like when reading the end of the gospel of Mark, I am holding my breath, "what happens next?" I commend Tri and Nancy Robinson's strong clarion call to truth.

Larry Pew, D. Min

"This is an excellent book. It has brought to me an understanding of how we Christians went from praying to God to relying on a political party to solve our nation's problems... I was alive and active in the church during this transition to politics. Yet my focus was on the local church. This book explains what was happening to the American church and why. It is a must read for all who call themselves Christians. At the very least, it will help them to understand the forces that have changed and molded the church. Do any of us actually believe that our country can stand without a direct and mighty intervention of God?"

Duncan Trunnell

"...when someone (like Tri) points out generational differences and champions the strengths in our current Millennial culture, that is when an opportunity arises to grab the baton you've been handed and run your portion of the race. My prayer, as a Millennial, is that we will rise to the challenge of our age and partner with a powerful move of God that reaches the world for Jesus."

Danial Dean,
Australian Millennial

Tri Robinson's important new book shows that meeting the complicated demands of today's world, particularly the environmental degradation that is accelerating with every passing year, represents a fulfilment of our Christianity, namely coming together to bring justice and compassion to the world with love, joy, peace, patience, kindness, goodness, faithfulness and self-control, ultimately putting others before self and preserving the inheritance of future generations. If we can rise to the challenges of the world around us we will find maturity. Tri warns that American Evangelicals have drifted away from engagement with too many issues for partisan reasons, and in doing so have appeared callous and have driven people away from Christ. This is a book that can change the way you see the world, and shows that the Christian life is active and compelling, not passive, entrenched and combative. Tri writes prophetically about a future where a new generation engages with Christianity in a fresh way, not shrinking from the huge threats that humanity faces, but meeting them and coming into their own with Christ. Christians talk about being left behind. If you don't want to be left behind, then read this book.

Will Frazier,
Award-winning documentary producer

RE:FORM

THE DECLINE OF AMERICAN
EVANGELICALISM AND A PATH
FOR THE NEW GENERATION
TO RE:FORM THEIR FAITH

Tri Robinson

Timber Butte Publishing
Sweet, Idaho

Table of Contents

Dedication

To my granddaughter, Hope Colleen, a true Millennial, who has motivated her grandmother and me to better understand her generation. Because of her sincere and unique perspective of the Christian faith, she has given us new hope for the future of the church.

Acknowledgments

Nancy, my wife and best friend, recently told me she believed Re:Form is the message of my life and the book I was always meant to write. Without her support and encouragement, it is a message I may never have had the fortitude to complete. Besides Nancy, I would like to acknowledge so many people who contributed their gifting and passion to the process of seeing that this message would find its way to publication.

I must acknowledge Kevin and Ginny Thienes who didn't merely bring their editing skills to the table, but a realistic understanding and love for the church, a deep concern for the Millennial generation, and unique prophetic insight.

To Mitchell Maldonado, a creative millennial who designed the book's cover.

I want to express my appreciation for Jason Chatraw who years ago coined the word Re:Form. It was Jason who convinced me I had messages worthy of putting into print.

I want to thank Trevor and Andrea Estes, and all the Vineyard staff and volunteers who have so diligently and successfully carried on the work of the Vineyard Christian Fellowship of Boise, developing it as a church possessing a sincere heart that constantly reflects the compassionate and merciful heart of Jesus.

My thanks also to Alexei Laushklin, founder & Executive Director, Kingdom Mission Society, and so many others who were willing to pre-read my unedited manuscript, giving valued input and encouragement whether they shared its political perspective or not. Thanks to those who wrote reviews and endorsements, many of which brought tears to my eyes.

Thank you, Will Frazier, for committing seven years of your life producing the ninety-minute documentary "American Creation / Preacher and Cowboy" on Timber Butte Homestead, a documentary which followed Nancy's and my life for the sake of communicating this message on film.

And my thanks to Kate, Brook, and Andrea, my Gen X children who not only helped form my thinking on this subject, but encouraged me to be bold and honest.

And my thanks to Pat Armstrong, more like a brother but a dear old friend, who allows me to rant and rave at the world's decaying condition while at the same time keeping me centered in the miracle of God's creation and plan.

What is RE:FORM?

Re:Form speaks of a "new form" of authentic Christian expression. It will be an emerging form of Christian faith birthed by a new generation who are in reaction to the conservative, right-wing ideology of American Evangelicalism. *Re:Form* is the story of how and why this new form of Christian life will occur.

Re:Form is written in three parts: "What Was," "What Is," and "What Will Be." Part one, "What Was," looks back into church history and church culture focusing primarily on the Jesus Movement revival of the 1960s and 1970s, while also reflecting on historical cycles of events which helped spawn the Protestant Reformation and the Great Awakening revivals. The second part, "What Is," looks at the conditions surrounding past revivals and compares them with the present day. It illuminates the political and cultural climate in today's world with characteristics that birthed these other past revivals. It shows how the culture's fears and frustrations of the 2000-teens are like those of the 1960s, but on steroids. The thesis being, America is ripe for a new wave of spiritual awakening. Part three, "What Will Be," provides prophetic insight as to what that awakening might look like: The Millennial generation rising up, much as the Baby Boomers did in the '60s, bringing *Re:Form* into American culture as an authentic expression of Christian faith

The title *Re:Form* is not a new thought to me. For over sixteen years, I have tried to use my influence as an Evangelical pastor of a larger American church to revitalize values of social justice, creation care, and other ministries of compassion and justice back into the Evangelical structure and culture. Early on, I had begun a ministry that addressed these issues which was given the name *Re:Form* by a comrade of mine, Jason Chatraw. Jason had co-written four books with me in the early 2000s — *Saving God's Green Earth; Small Footprint, Big Handprint; Revolutionary Leadership;* and *Jesus in the Mirror.*

It is my belief that one day an emerging generation will grasp the biblical values of environmental degradation as it relates to the world's extreme poor, and other issues of social injustice, such as human trafficking, human inequality, civil rights, and the rejection of foreign aliens. This generation will become the champions for the downtrodden. I know, however, in order for this to occur, they will likely rebel against the Evangelical system in which many had been raised, just as Baby Boomers had rebelled against their culture's traditions. This will happen when they perceive

Evangelicalism as an agency of extreme right-wing politics that outwardly opposes issues of climate change and social justice. As American Evangelicalism loses its effectiveness in a secular world as a trusted communicator of the compassionate love of God, its influence as an agency of faith will fade, inspiring something fresh and new to emerge, taking its place. My belief is that the time for this is just around the corner.

A Word about RE:FORM from a Millennial

Tri Robinson's most recent book, *Re:Form*, presents an engaging, challenging and thought-provoking discussion on the history of the American Evangelical tradition and the need for the new Millennial generation to reform and renew their faith.

The book tackles this topic by looking at the three themes of "What was", "What is" and "What will be". The first two sections give the historical context of Evangelicalism and explain how churches have historically adapted to the needs of their time, encouraged by prophetic voices and inspired by God. Tri outlines this history in a clear and succinct way whilst also giving good explanations for the reasons why the Evangelical church has slowly given less emphasis to the issues of climate change and social justice that are so important to the Millennial generation.

Tri explains how Evangelicalism in the USA is now commonly equated with right-wing politics and that the Millennial generation is experiencing a "cultural disjuncture" as they witness the disparity between professed Christian values (such as looking after the poor) and supposedly "Christian" politics.

Reading this book helped me to better understand not only the spiritual and historical context of the church in America but also the need for a move of God to bring spiritual renewal, spearheaded by Millennials, that is relevant and impacting for our generation.

As a member of the Millennial generation, I can relate to the feelings Tri describes of confusion and frustration that living in the current cultural and political climate creates. However, the third and final section of his book illuminated to me the way in which God may move to draw people to himself by using Millennials to bring about significant change in the current culture, including the areas that we feel the church has often overlooked: social justice and environmental care.

Tri's book was an accessible and insightful read, a mix of story, warning, challenge and hope. Reading it has caused me to look more seriously at the state of the world and further ignited the desire in me to see and be part of this generation's spiritual Re:Form.

Kara Dean

Danial and Kara Dean are an Australian Millennial couple whom recently traveled the globe, dedicating a year of their marriage to seeking out and participating with Christian organizations committed to justice and compassion ministry.

Part I

WHAT WAS

Prelude to Awakening

End of the Ages

I can remember the day well. It was summer on the old Robinson ranch and I was totally focused on building a rock generator house about a hundred yards from the old ranch house. I was a school teacher at the time, but always dedicated my two-and-a-half-month summer breaks to getting things done on the old place. The ranch had been in our family for four generations but no one had taken up full- time residence since WWII. It required every bit of my spare time just to make it livable for my young family. Nancy, my bride, was twenty-one at the time and pregnant with our first child.

I had just mixed a fresh batch of concrete in a wheelbarrow and was about to set a large, flat, granite rock chest high on the wall I was building when I heard the cabin's screen door open and swing shut. Our ranch was in the middle of nowhere and no one was around except the two of us. The urgent footsteps I heard coming up behind me couldn't have been anyone else's but Nancy's. I can't express what a cute, young, pregnant mother she was. She was the joy of my life; everything a young man could have desired for a bride. We were living the dream so many of our generation idealistically desired in the 1970s. Together, we were developing a sustainable homestead on raw, unblemished land far from the hectic lifestyle of the cities. As I turned to greet her, not only did I notice she had been crying, I saw real fear in her eyes.

Before I go on, let me quickly recap some of the events which had transpired over the previous months. First of all, the old ranch was isolated. It was located on the side of a mountain on the western end of the Mojave Desert, an hour's drive from the nearest real town. Our closest neighbors were a mile to our west, and four miles to the east. We had neither a telephone nor electricity and our water was spring fed from the canyon behind the cabin. When I went off to my teaching job in the city each day, Nancy stayed on the ranch, giving her many hours alone to think about her life. Being the daughter of a Navy Commander, she grew up in the San Diego area with three siblings and tons of friends. Like most young girls, her life had been full. Before her solitary time on the old ranch, she never had so many quiet hours to contemplate life and her role in it. It was in the midst of this unique season, living in nature and solitude, that she came to a realization of God's existence and presence. In her hunger to know Him better, she started to read the Bible and listen to whatever Christian station she could locate on our battery-powered transistor radio.

A second factor that made this day significant was something that was going on in the culture of the day. During the late 1960s and into the 1970s, there was a spiritual phenomenon irrupting in our generation known as the Jesus Movement. The Jesus Movement was a Christian revival unique for its day, but significant for many years to come. I'll say more about this later, but one of the things that characterized this unique spiritual awakening was its heavy emphasis on eschatology. Eschatology is a study of the last days, or the end times. It is a prophetic perspective concerning how the world as we know it will one day come to an end. There's a reason that eschatology became such a big deal in those days and as this story moves into our present day, we'll better understand how it helps set the stage for the potential of a great spiritual awakening in the 21st century.

> * * *
>
> Exposing people to eschatology, as it was being presented, was an effective way of literally scaring the hell out of people and showing them why they needed a relationship with God.
>
> * * *

Along with this emphasis on eschatology, the Jesus Movement was theologically Evangelical, which meant (at least at that time) it focused heavily on evangelism. That is to say, due to the passion and a sense of urgency all of us were feeling, evangelism was an all-consuming focus. In the 1970s, a number of books were written about the last days and some scary low-budget movies were produced in an effort to illuminate the seriousness of it. Exposing people to eschatology, as it was being presented, was an effective way of literally scaring the hell out of people and showing them why they needed a relationship with God. One of the most famous books written in that day was called, *The Late Great Planet Earth,* by Hal Lindsey. It was published in the epicenter of the Jesus Movement in 1970 and became the bestselling book that year.

That day on the old ranch, the day Nancy came out to find me with tears in her eyes, was the day she finished reading Hal Lindsey's book. She was so upset it took me several minutes to find out what had happened.

I remember being really concerned, not understanding the reason for her tears. Even while my freshly mixed concrete was drying in the hot summer sun, I dropped what I was doing, took off my gloves and pulled her to me. "What's wrong?" I asked. She melted into me and began to sob, unable to speak for several minutes. Being pregnant, her emotions were often fragile, but this day I knew there had to be something powerful driving them. Something must have happened. "What is it?" I asked.

"I've been reading that book again," she said. "The book by that man Hal Lindsey everyone is reading, *The Late Great Planet Earth.*" Then she said, with another burst of emotion, "I'm so afraid!"

"What are you so afraid of?" I asked. "I thought you said it was a Christian book."

With that, she began telling me all she had been learning: about end time prophecies and how the earth and everything on it was going to burn up, how Jesus was going to return and take His people up into heaven for eternity, and how everything else would be destroyed. There was a lot more to it, but for me the whole thing sounded crazy. She acted as if it was all going to happen in the next week or month. For her, at that moment, the idea of building a home and farm to live on and even more so, having a baby and starting a new family was a terrifying thought. Why would Jesus, a God of love, want to take all that away? It was a devastating thought for a young mother about to have her first baby.

In retrospect, I'm sure my reaction was not the best. It wasn't a reaction to bring peace to a young woman in a grave moment of distress. The fact is, it made me really mad! I would be the first to tell you I didn't know a whole lot about the Bible or even the nature of God, but I had been raised in church and the story she was telling me didn't sound like the Jesus I had known growing up. Nancy's hunger to know God was way ahead of mine. We had just started to attend church again after six years of university life, while starting a new teaching job, and spending every extra waking minute rebuilding our farmstead. I went because it was important to Nancy more than feeling a deep need for spirituality myself. I was just trying to be a good husband and keep peace in the family.

"That's crazy," I said. "Where in the Bible does it say any of that? I don't know too much about Bible prophecy," I said, "but what you're telling me doesn't sound much like a God of love."

Nancy was running more on emotion than biblical knowledge. In her urgency to get me to understand how scary it all was, she unloaded all she had been learning about the book of Revelation, Daniel, and other Old Testament prophets and how it was all being fulfilled right before our eyes, especially in present-day Israel. It was all scrambled and made little sense to me.

A few weeks later, while I was trying to untangle the confusion I was feeling, my mom and dad dropped by the ranch for a weekend visit. My dad was approaching retirement age and was probably feeling his years. He was a practical person and a man of traditional faith. I remember him looking at me and saying, "Well, one thing I know for sure, we're all in our last days. Some of us more than others (referring to himself). We're all going to be with Jesus one way or another." Then he said, "Maybe He's coming down or we're going up, but we should live in a state of readiness either way."

Now that made sense to me. It lifted some of the mystery off of the matter, at least for a while, anyway. Nancy and I attended a very Jesus Movement-type church throughout the '70s and beyond. In the early days, we heard dozens of messages about the end times and sat through many studies on prophecy and the Book of Revelation. Some of it was good, but much was overly radical, giving personal views and interpretations of biblical prophecy that I now look back at and shake my head, wondering how Evangelicalism survived that crazy season. Many evenings, our generation sat in nontraditional church auditoriums, which were characteristic of those Jesus Movement days, watching scary apocalyptic movies shown on reel-to-reel sixteen millimeter projectors, movies like *A Thief in the Night*, *A Distant Thunder*, *Image of the Beast*, and others. Night after night, as the movies ended, dozens of people committed their lives to the Lord in hopes of being raptured before the wrath would fall on sinful man. It was a wild time for sure! Everyone was debating when the so-called "rapture" would happen and who would be left behind and who would go. This started many discussions concerning authentic salvation and what a person had to do to obtain what was being called "fire insurance." There were also ongoing arguments concerning the great tribulation or the time of tribulation. This spoke of a time of great human suffering, which was to occur around the time of Christ's second coming and would last for seven years. New theologies, or more accurately, new theories, arose concerning when the rapture would occur during the time of tribulation. These theories were based on people's perspective of Scripture and their understanding of the nature of God, and in some cases, hopeful thinking. Some were adamant that Christians would miss the seven-year tribulation, having been raptured before this time. Others said the rapture would happen after the tribulation, while still others were confident it would be in the midst of it. New terminology came into the Christian vocabulary. Words, such as pre-trib, mid-trib, and post-trib reflected these views and for some people, became hills to die on. Sadly, more than one church split occurred because of such disagreements. The same kinds of debate arose over what was referred to as the millennium. This was a word that, although not occurring in Scripture, referred to a thousand-year rule of Christ at His second coming. When the millennium was to occur also created discord and anger among Evangelicals who were desperately trying to figure all this out.

As a young Christian, I couldn't figure out why it all had to be so complicated, confusing, and create so much disagreement among believers who professed they desired unity in the Body of Christ. Once during that time, a man prophesied over me saying God was going to give me a divine ability to unravel the mysteries of the Bible so that people could not only understand His heart for them, but His plan for His world. I took those words to heart. For the past forty years, it has been amazing to see how His grace and power has enabled me to help people understand who He is and what He desires for His people to do.

Once, while I was trying to figure all this end times stuff out, I remember stumbling on two different passages that got me thinking. One was in 1 Corinthians and the other in the Book of Hebrews. In Corinthians, Paul was talking about how events and stories in the Old Testament were given as examples and warnings for us who live in the "end of the ages" so that we will stand firm and not stumble. I recognized the term "end of the ages" from Matthew 24 where Jesus told his disciples about events that would usher in "the close of the ages." The author of Hebrews said a similar thing to Paul's words in Corinthians where he spoke of Christ's sacrifice saying it was once and for all. It didn't have to be repeated over and over again like the sacrifices of the Old Testament. He said, *"...he has appeared once for all at the end of the ages to do away with sin by the sacrifice of himself"* (Hebrews 9:6, ESV). Wow, this was huge for me! What Paul and the author of Hebrews were saying was that the end of the age, or the last days, actually began at the resurrection of Jesus. God's Kingdom had come to earth as it is in heaven at that moment. In other words, we don't have to guess when the last days will come; we are living in them now and will be until His second coming. Granted, things are going to get a lot more intense just before His second coming, much like birth pangs before a mother's delivery.

As crazy as the '70s were, especially when it came to this issue of eschatology among the Evangelical Christian world, for many it was the beginning of what became a sincere and authentic walk with God. For young leaders like Nancy and me, it was the beginning of a life of meaningful ministry which would one day reach into cities across the nation and around the world serving thousands of broken people. In many cases, this growing movement would, over time, reach and serve the poorest of the world's poor. It would lead us into a rich and meaningful journey that we would never regret.

Looking back to see forward

The question you might be asking is, why look back sixty years to events that happened in the 1960s and '70s in a discussion concerning the last days? King Solomon once said, "...There's nothing new under the sun" (Ecclesiastes 1:9, ESV). which is another way of saying that history has a strange way of repeating itself even when we look back and identify the mistakes made in the past. Not only that, but the events leading up to the last days' scenario will one day create a social climate for an anti-Christ to rise to power. Jesus warned that these social conditions would birth the potential for widespread deception, even for those who perceive themselves as strong people of faith. These conditions will not pop out of thin air, but will be symptomatic of a culture that has slowly eroded to a tipping point. In fact, we could make a case that the start button of the last days' time bomb was in the book of Genesis and has been ticking at an ever-increasing cadence since. For the sake of keeping this book to a readable length, I'll start my story at the beginning of the Baby Boomer generation.

The Times they "were" a changing!

Bob Dylan was prophetically singing, "The Times They Are A-Changin'," in the 1960s, which reflected the feelings the Baby Boomer generation was having. Feelings, that if not spoken as passionately as they were in the '60s, are certainly being felt with greater intensity by the Millennials as our culture rapidly approaches 2020. Not only that, but as some have said, Dylan's lyrics, written in 1963, are equally prophetic for today. Dylan wrote about the waters growing so much that we might become drenched to the bone! Was Dylan talking about the phenomena of storm surge and a changing climate or were they just poetic words? One thing I know for sure, our world was in a state of rapid change in the '60s and that set the stage for a spiritual revival.

Events and conditions in the '60s tilled the cultural soil for revival:

- **Mistrust of government leadership**

Dylan was verbalizing the uncertainty the Boomer generation was feeling and for good reasons. For the first time, there was deep mistrust of our government. They had sent our young men into a war most of our generation didn't support. Our friends were dying in the far-away jungles of Vietnam for reasons we couldn't understand. At the same time, events that surrounded the Watergate scandal reinforced our beliefs that we couldn't trust the words and motives of our national leaders and political system. The nation's African American communities had had enough of segregation and social injustice, and the anger, rage, and fear our generation felt erupted like a great volcano.

- **The fear of global environmental decline**

The world really was changing as Dylan had proclaimed. In the 1960s, the Boomer generation inhabited college and university campuses across the nation. We were in a season of intellectual inquiry, looking closely at the world we lived in. We could see our world in a state of decline and it alarmed us. One of the greatest surges of what would become the environmental movement began as a result. The classic folk music being composed, books being written, and movies being produced were not only addressing and exposing the problems, but stimulating the fear. One such book was written in 1968 by a professor at Stanford University. Paul Ehrlich, along with his wife, Anne, exposed the threat of overpopulation and advocated immediate action to slow it down in their bestselling book, *The Population Bomb*.

• Overpopulation

The Population Bomb was a warning of doom. It spoke of overpopulation, mass starvation of humans, and drastic social change in the coming years. In some ways, it verbalized what many of us were already feeling. The Baby Boomer generation was primarily a post WWII generation. I am a perfect example. I was born in 1948. Just prior to 1950, the world population reached 2.3 billion people. This may not seem too alarming at first glance, but when you consider it took from the beginning of human history until the Industrial Revolution in the later part of the 1800s to reach a world population of just 1 billion people, it shed new light on things (It is debatable how many years that was, but no matter your view on creation, it took a long time to get that many folks on planet Earth). Then, from about 1850 to 1948, less than 100 years, the population grew another billion. A graph illustrating this trend might look like the shape of a hockey stick that jettisons upward in a vertical line starting just before 1900. By the time *The Population Bomb* was written in 1968, the population reached 3.5 billion; another billion people in our lifetime and we, as a generation, were barely adults. Not only that, but when the book had reached its greatest point of popularity in 1972, the population had climbed yet another half billion. Making matters even more alarming, the Ehrlichs predicted it could reach eight billion during our lifetime. It's remarkable how accurate their prediction was considering it is now 2017 and the population has grown to nearly 7.5 billion — and many Boomers are still here to see it come true. Besides the rapid growth, one of the most alarming parts of the Ehrlichs' warning was that if the population reached eight billion, the earth would become unsustainable and enter a time of rapid environmental decline, causing global human suffering.

- **A response of anger stimulates movements of activism, protests, and riots**

The *Population Bomb* sounded an alarm and demanded a thrust toward national and global environmental reformation. This gave a second book written a few years later, *The Monkey Wrench Gang* (which later became a movie), a lot of attention as well. *The Monkey Wrench Gang* was a novel written by Edward Abbey. As with the Ehrlichs' writing, it raised controversy as it told the story of a group of environmentalists who used sabotage as a means of protest, damaging machinery used to destroy wild lands and wilderness. Our generation didn't need encouragement to physically fight for what we thought was ethically right, especially when it came to issues like the environment and civil rights. An example would be the establishment of Green Peace in 1971. Its zealous members physically engaged in issues like climate change, deforestation, over- fishing of ocean waters, commercial whaling, and nuclear proliferation. These young activists were so committed to their cause that they literally put their lives in harm's way as a means of protest. In a less radical way, the Sierra Club, which had been established in 1892 by John Muir, took on new life under the leadership of Michael McCloskey in the '60s and '70s. Through his leadership, the Sierra Club members managed to save the Grand Canyon from exploitation, established the Redwoods National Park, and fought for legislation against such things as strip mining and air pollution. They became a powerful political force against efforts to damage our nation's natural beauty. All this resulted because of the turmoil the Boomer generation was experiencing, but for whatever good happened, a lot of dysfunction emerged as well. Many turned to angry protests that sometimes had devastating results. One such case was a student massacre in 1970 on the Kent State campus. The Ohio National Guard was called to police what was meant to be a peaceful student protest against the expansion of the Vietnam War into Cambodia. As the students reacted to resistance, four students were shot and killed while nine others were wounded. Student outrage broke out across the nation, causing hundreds of university, college, and high school campuses to close while four million young people walked out of classes and staged protests of their own. Kent State was just one example of many dozens of political demonstrations staged at the end of the '60s and beginning of the '70s, which rose up out of a generation that demanded social change.

- ## A fight for civil rights for Black America

At the same time college students were protesting on the steps of capitol buildings, Black Americans reached their boiling point concerning the injustice they had endured since the days of slavery. John F. Kennedy had called for the Civil Rights Act of 1964, giving all Americans equal rights to be served in facilities open to the public without discrimination based on race. This included hotels, restaurants, schools, theaters, and retail stores as well as greater protection when it came to voting. The southern states, especially, had become so entrenched in segregation that a cultural change of such magnitude couldn't happen by legislation alone. As Blacks tried to exercise their newly granted freedoms, there was great resistance and an increase in racial tension. This instigated violent protests and rioting. Black men were especially vulnerable to white brutality from police forces and racist organizations like the Klu Klux Klan. In reaction to an act of police brutality to a young black man in Los Angeles, an argument broke out which quickly escalated into what became known as the Watts Riots. 4,000 members of the California National Guard were called in to aid the Los Angeles Police Department in quenching the outbreak, which resulted in 34 deaths and $40 million worth of damage. Events like this, as well as inspiration from leaders, such as Malcom X, promoted the Black Power movement, and in 1966, the formation of a group called the Black Panthers. This group of young black people believed that passive protests would not do enough to awaken the country to their plight and took up arms to fight for their rights.

It became evident that violent resistance just created more violence. Then, a loud, clear voice began to resonate among the black multitudes. That voice was Martin Luther King, Jr. a Baptist preacher who advocated nonviolent civil disobedience based on Christian beliefs. God won the day and Christian values became the ultimate answer to hundreds of years of strife. Things got better for the American black community, but the battle for equality was far from over.

- **Women's liberation and the Feminist movement**

While Blacks were fighting against discrimination, women all across America were also fighting for equality. They fought against sexual discrimination when it came to equal pay and position in the work place. Thousands of women marched in the streets of Washington and protested on capitol steps. In the early 1960s, most women were spending up to 55 hours a week doing domestic chores, such as housekeeping and child rearing. Very few were accepted in many professional fields other than teaching school, nursing, and secretarial work. As a result, a second wave of women's suffrage broke out, becoming known as the Feminist Movement or the Women's Liberation Movement. By the late '60s and early '70s, these women not only broke the silence, but began winning a new place of respect in American society. Some protests won media attention when women publicly burned their bras, which added even more paint to the images that made the '60s a time of colorful new beginnings. All these events, birthed throughout the '60s, God used to stimulate a spiritual awakening.

- **New revolutions of drugs and sex are born**

While some turned outward in public protest, others turned inward, finding temporary relief from their feelings of disillusionment and despair with self-medication. Soon, the excessive use of marijuana and stronger hallucinogenic drugs became common place and spawned a drug culture unprecedented in our nation's history.

A new lifestyle of liberation arose in places like the Haight-Ashbury district of San Francisco, birthing what became known as the Hippie or Flower Child movement. Not only were drugs becoming the medication of the day, but a whole new morality emerged — a sexual revolution. The words "Free Love" became the cry and the slogan "If it feels good — do it" became yet another form of protest. If the world was coming to an end, then who cared?

- **A hunger and surge for spirituality**

Some turned inward for relief, while others turned outward looking to spirituality for answers. Our culture was in a state of disjuncture; everything felt upside down and backwards, and for many there seemed nowhere to turn but to God — yes, to God, but not to the religion of our parents.

Because of deep feelings of concern for an uncertain future, yet another reaction emerged; a search for the true meaning of life. In our quest, not everybody chose Jesus as the answer. In those days, I had a friend named Charley, with whom I ran track and cross country throughout my high school days in Southern California. Charley had great talent as a runner, but was a little unstable. Soon after graduation, he ran off to India in search of a Hindu Guru. He wanted answers and was willing to go to the other side of the world to find them. Crazy as it may seem now, this level of radical hunger wasn't uncommon. I was later told he ended up dying of an overdose of heroin. That has always troubled me. I wish I would have known enough at the time to help him toward a better journey.

Most of us knew little of God. Many, if not most, had some exposure to church life in our childhood, but left it behind as soon as we were old enough to escape the desires of well-meaning parents. Nancy had been raised in an Irish Catholic family and I had been raised Protestant Presbyterian. The first real conversation we ever had together was about our faith. She was a college freshman and I was a senior, so she naturally thought I'd have answers for her many questions. Her sister had just converted to the Jehovah Witness religion and had told her the world would come to an end in 1975. Nancy was scared and confused. I'm not sure I had much comfort for her. My knowledge of God was a convoluted mix of Sunday school flannel graphs and four years of secular college professors.

* * *

My knowledge of God was a convoluted mix of Sunday school flannel graphs and four years of secular college professors.

* * *

When we made the decision to get married, Nancy's parents requested that we receive counseling from a Catholic priest in our small college town. In more recent years, I have met some really wonderful Catholic priests, but this guy was old school and had zero grace or tolerance for someone he felt certain was destined for hell. It wasn't just in

Ireland that the Catholics and Protestants didn't see eye to eye in those days. He told Nancy she would go to hell if she married me, which ended our first counseling appointment. Like so many of our generation, we decided we were going to have to figure this God thing out on our own, which was the very thing that birthed the Jesus Movement.

Eschatology answered the question

I think there are a number of significant points to consider concerning what gave the Jesus Movement such distinctiveness and jet-propelled momentum:

- When thousands of young people came searching for a relationship with God, the leaders they discovered and gravitated toward were Evangelicals. This will have more meaning as my story unfolds in relationship to the subject of the last days.
- Those who came were hungry to have two questions answered: What's going to happen to this world that seems to be coming to an end? What's going to happen to me when it does?

Eschatology answered the first question and redemption answered the second: God had a plan for our world, a world we believed was moving toward crisis. For those who accepted His existence and put their faith in His divine nature, there was not destruction but eternal redemption.

- The third thing to understand was that the Jesus Movement was birthed in a time of great rebellion. We wanted Jesus, but we wanted Him on our own terms and in our own way. We rejected religion as we perceived it, pushing back from the trappings of our parent's faith.

One of the great early leaders of the Jesus movement was a man by the name of Chuck Smith, who later became the founding pastor of Calvary Chapel. Although Chuck had his roots in the Baptist church, he was wise enough not to try to make Baptists out of the radical young people who asked him for sound Bible teaching. He also knew that they had been rejected from the traditional mainline Christian churches because of their long hair, torn up clothes, and unwillingness to wear shoes or sit in chairs. He knew they wouldn't come to a traditional church facility, so he and other like-minded leaders opened up gymnasiums and warehouses for larger meetings, allowing them to sit on the floor. They also baptized the new believers in the ocean, avoiding the traditional church baptismal.

31 flavors of Christianity

I didn't fully commit my life to God until the Jesus Movement had been under way for a while. It was sometime toward the end of the 1970s, but when I did I had no affiliation to any denomination or any defined group. I came to Jesus because I had a very real personal encounter with Him and because of it, couldn't deny His existence. He made Himself real to me and authentically changed me. When the Apostle Paul told us in Romans 12 to present our bodies as a sacrifice—alive, holy, and pleasing to God—and *"Do not be conformed to this present world, but be transformed by the renewing of your mind, so that you may test and approve what is the will of God— what is good and well-pleasing and perfect"* (Romans 12:2, NET), that's exactly what happened to me. My mind was transformed; it was completely changed. I had a brand-new world view and because of it, all I wanted to do was discover His perfect will for my life. What I didn't know was how easy it would be to let religious trappings derail my desire for a simple faith and love for Him. I didn't know how convoluted and confusing religion could be.

I had never heard the word "Evangelical" at that point of my journey and honestly had no idea of what the word meant. I didn't realize that the Jesus Movement had its roots planted in it and wouldn't have known if that was a good or bad thing. I did know that there were different categories of the Christian faith. I knew that the two main divisions were Roman Catholicism and Protestantism. I also knew that among the Catholics there were many different Orders and among the Protestants there were several different types of Christian expression. There were Pentecostals, churches like the Assembly of God and Four Square, who emphasized an emotional experience with the Holy Spirit. There were also mainline churches much like the church I had grown up in, such as Presbyterian, Lutheran, and Methodist (my great-grandfather had been a

Methodist circuit preacher). The mainline churches were the result of huge revivals from the distant past, like the Reformation, which started Protestantism, and the Great Awakening. Then there was yet a third group, also under the Protestant umbrella, whose primary focus was on the accuracy of the Bible. Knowing God for them was a higher value than experiencing His presence like the Pentecostals did. Baptists would be an example of this group, who I later discovered were called Evangelicals.

I couldn't understand why a Christian wasn't just a Christian and why the Body of Christ had been divided so many times. The group of Christians we joined referred to themselves as "Non-denominational." That sounded like a great idea to me and to many of my fellow new believers. We wanted a pure and simple relationship with God without traditional rituals, overly organized, or rigid doctrine that we recognized had a way of sucking the life out of faith. I'll admit we were naïve. We had little or no knowledge of church history and thus couldn't understand how the church had splintered into so many factions so many times. The funny part was, we all just become Evangelicals without knowing it, or even knowing what one was.

So, what's an Evangelical?

One thing I've learned as I studied the matter of Christian revival is that God has a way of keeping His church not only alive, but in a constant state of growth. I observed that throughout Church history there were extremely dark times, but out of the darkness God would raise up new leaders. He would breathe a freshening of His Spirit upon people to enable another surge of life. In that way, the church would experience an awakening and revival which would result in the birthing of a new expression of the Christian faith. Often, this would eventually be identified as a denomination. At the beginning of the great Protestant Reformation in the 1500s, God used Martin Luther in such a way.

Luther was a young Catholic Priest who discovered, through his reading of Scripture, how far the Catholic Church had strayed from authentic faith. He realized that Catholicism had totally lost its way and had evolved into a controlling, political, spiritually-dead organization. Putting his life on the line, he spoke out against the heresy he had observed and grew to despise. Through his efforts, he translated the Bible into the language of the common people so they, for the first time, could read the Bible and discover God on their own. This was revolutionary at that time and began a major change in the culture, resulting in breaking away from Catholicism and the beginning of the Protestant faith. The first branch of this new expression was, of course, Lutheranism. The Lutheran denomination is the remnant of that courageous event, which took place more than five hundred years ago.

Another example, and a more relevant one when it comes to our understanding of Evangelicalism, was the Wesleyan revival in the mid-1700s. In many ways, the same spiritual deadness was taking place in the Church of England. It is clear that spiritual deadness was not just a Catholic problem, but a Protestant one as well; however, neither is a problem for God. As God used Luther two hundred years before to reform the Catholic faith, He used John Wesley and his contemporaries to reform the Protestant faith. Like the Catholic church in Luther's time, the Church of England had also become a politically controlling entity in Wesley's time.

Wesley took Christianity to the streets of England during a time of great social despair. Like Luther, he revealed the truth of the Gospel to the multitudes after being expelled from the Church of England. Because the persecution he received was so great, in the beginning of his ministry he stood on his father's grave to preach, as it was the only piece of real-estate the Church of England couldn't control. The Wesleyan revival spread rapidly around the world with the leadership of a number of other powerful preachers and became known later as the Great Awakening. Several things characterized Wesley's ministry:

- His very clear presentation of the Gospel message.
- His belief that people needed to make a personal commitment to Christ, accompanied by repentance, in order to enter into an authentic relationship with Jesus.
- He believed the gospel consisted of the doctrine of salvation by grace through faith in Jesus's atonement. This later was referred to as a "Born Again" experience.
- He believed the preaching of the gospel should be in the hands of the common man. As a result, he created a method by which

he could train hundreds of young men to take the gospel all over England and around the world (A side note was that my great-grandfather was one of those young men. His name was John Wesley Robinson and he planted many churches across the western American frontier).

- Wesley's methods were so effective the movement he began was called "Methodist." The Methodist churches of today are the remnant of his work.

The foundation of Wesley's beliefs concerning the way to salvation became the foundation of "Evangelicalism." This spread beyond the Methodist church, becoming the doctrine of many protestant faiths. Today, there are nearly three million Evangelicals worldwide, which comprises about thirteen percent of the total Christian population.

A New Song

The Bible tells us that as the world begins to wind down it will experience what Jesus called "birth pangs," which will be manifested in an escalation of environmental crises, a global increase in violence, and the rising up of an antichrist. At the same time, the Bible tells us there will be a surge of worldwide evangelism whereby the gospel will be preached to every nation. This, then, indicates the evidence of one final Christian awakening.

Historically, we know that revivals are sadly unrecognized and missed by the established dominant religious system of the time. In fact, the existing system persecutes through extreme negativity the spark of new life that emerges. This happened by the Catholic Church in the Reformation, by the Church of England in the Great Awakening, and, in a lesser way, by the mainline churches at the beginning of the Jesus Movement.

* * *

For me, it would be tragic for someone like myself, who had dedicated most of their adult life to leading an Evangelical church, to not only miss something special God was doing in my time but instead become a persecutor of it.

* * *

To be honest, that's always concerned me given my understanding of church history. For me, it would be tragic for someone like myself, who had dedicated most of their adult life to leading an Evangelical church, to not only miss something special God was doing in my time but instead become a persecutor of it. My prayer has always been, "Lord, please show me what to look for so I'll not miss Your fresh new touch on humanity. Help me to recognize it, embrace it, and not push back on it."

One of the distinguishing signs of every new move of God is what might be called, "a new song." The new song I'm speaking of was characteristic of all three examples we've been illuminating — through the ministry of Martin Luther, John and Charles Wesley, and even during the Jesus Movement. In all three cases, there were major surges of creativity, not only with music but in all forms of the arts. As the creator of the universe, God is a creative God, and where His hand moves His people reflect this characteristic.

Martin Luther was a flutist and song writer who believed that not only should the Scripture be in the hands of common people, but music as well. Prior to the Reformation, music was primarily melodious Latin chants performed by priests and monks. Luther believed all men should participate in the activity of musical praise. At one point Luther wrote, "Next to the word of God, the noble art of music is the greatest treasure in the world. It controls our hearts, minds, and spirits. A person who does not regard music as a marvelous creation of God does not deserve to be called a human being; he should be permitted to hear nothing but the braying of asses and the grunting of hogs!" While the Catholic church was chanting in Latin, Luther was writing hymns, such as "A Mighty Fortress is Our God" in the common language of the people. This restored congregational singing in the church.

The Wesley brothers, like Luther, were prolific song writers. They, too, wanted singing to move from choir lofts in cathedrals to the common people. The story is told that one of the radical things they did was to use lyrics, often taken from the Psalms, and put them to familiar pub room tunes of their day. This, too, made the singing of gospel music easy for the multitudes to learn and corporately sing, most likely with great gusto.

The Jesus Movement was birthed in the midst of the folk music revival of the '60s and '70s. Bob Dylan, Joan Baez, Peter, Paul and Mary,

James Taylor, Carol King, Simon and Garfunkel, Judy Collins and many, many others became household names and were used to shape and influence the culture of their day. As a young, unchurched generation emerged looking for new and creative ways to express their newfound love for God, they naturally embraced the music style of their generation. Almost every gathering of these young and zealous Christians included this whole new sound. Our music took a transition from the more traditional hymns of the churches we grew up in as we found ourselves singing more intimately to God rather than about God. I remember experiencing times when we gathered in various places and sang for long periods of time without ever looking at a written lyric because the music had become so familiar to everyone present. It had become a part of our lives and seemed to emerge from the depths of our souls as we regularly entered into glorious times of praising God together. We often entered into singing echoes in men and women's parts, and sometimes sang spontaneous harmonies that felt like they could only be Spirit inspired. We became lost in it with nothing but sincere hearts and an intense focus on God's presence.

The songs of the Jesus Movement had simple lyrics and memorable melodies. The kind of music you couldn't get off your mind. Over the course of time, things gradually became a bit more professional with tighter bands and more sophisticated music. It started to become increasingly more difficult to sing without lyrics being projected, which encouraged new believers to focus on a video screen rather than closing their eyes and looking to the Lord. It was a slow drift, but a steady one.

As a pastor and leader in a large Evangelical church, I began hearing groaning concerning the sound level of worship, the quality of sound systems, or the length of the worship time. That always grieved me because although the sound had changed through the years, I knew our worship leaders were absolutely devoted to the process with a deep desire to see the congregation become fully engaged.

The musicians and worship leaders of today's church have heard the tales concerning the fervency of worship during the Jesus Movement days and the Charismatic movement that accompanied it. They heard the stories from a remnant of Baby Boomers who were still longing for the old emotions and experiences that brought them so radically to Christ years before, forgetting that the Millennials hadn't even been born yet. In efforts to discover what they had missed, contemporary worship leaders often located and listened to old cassette recordings from forty years prior. I've listened to those recordings myself and although they may touch some old nostalgic memories, they frankly sound a bit corny even to me. I can understand why the younger ears of the new generation, used to high-level technology, might not be so enamored by it. The Jesus Movement is gone and to try to hang on to it, or any spiritual experience from the past, is only to miss what God wants to do in the future. We need hearts willing and ready to respond to the "new song." What we long for, only God can do. Only God can inhabit our song with a fresh presence of His Spirit. Our job as believers is to desperately want it and to patiently wait for it, knowing it may well be the ushering in of something new He is doing on the earth.

Renaissance: Surges of creativity accompanying spiritual awakening

It's not just fresh forms of music that accompany revivals and awakenings, but whole new surges of the arts and innovative thinking. Because these events happen over the course of time, they are not readily recognized as being connected, but looking in retrospect, reformation and renaissance have common denominators.

Five hundred years ago, the world emerged from a long season of darkness. That season was called the Dark Ages and it was characterized by superstition, oppressive religion, domineering lords, illiteracy, and basic primal existence. In the 14th century, a convergence occurred bringing the arts, music, education, science, creative innovation, and the Reformation altogether at once. It created a great synergistic collision of light, which ushered in the dawning of the Modern Age.

As only God could have it, the Protestant Reformation was remarkably birthed right in the midst of this swirl of new life. Leonardo da Vinci and Michelangelo revolutionized the arts, Gutenberg invented the printing press, Isaac Newton and Nicolaus Copernicus looked to science for discovery and understanding of the earth and the stars, while Greek scholars and philosophers attempted to answer the mysteries of the universe from humanistic perspectives. All this swirl of creativity, thought, and invention entered the world theater just as Luther brought reform to a dying religion. Luther, himself, was an inspirational scholar, innovator, and communicator and rather than pushing back and rejecting all that was occurring in his culture, he embraced it. The Catholic Church on the other hand, feeling threatened, aggressively reputed the sciences, fearing people would look to it for answers rather than placing their dependence on the church.

Luther saw the printing press as a provision from God for the purpose of spreading his message and providing Bibles for the common people. He used the arts to illustrate his teaching, and hymns and music as a new means of communication. Literacy rapidly spread in a society that desperately desired to read the Scripture he had translated and made available.

Reformation and Renaissance go hand in hand and although it will look different in the 21st century, it will surely rise in a culture experiencing turmoil and disjuncture. It will rise among a people longing for truth and answers to the conflict, fear, and uncertainty they will experience and feel.

The Charismatic renewal:
Preview of coming attractions

Another profound and strange phenomenon happened most intensely in the '70s and '80s. It became known around the world as the Charismatic Movement. Both Catholics and Protestants alike had the opportunity to experience a very real encounter with God, much like the apostles did on the day of Pentecost in Acts chapter two. I say "had the opportunity" because many rejected or denied it. I was there and will give testimony that it was very real.

There were a number of things that gave validity to the fact that God was authentically visiting His church during the time of the charismatic renewal. Night after night He came and renewed His people and manifested Himself in very outward physical ways. Ways that are hard to explain — you kind of had to be there. To describe the things we felt and saw would sound almost crazy if you personally didn't experience it. Being slain in the spirit for hours at a time, speaking in tongues when you said it couldn't be God or that it would never happen to you. These were common occurrences. Seeing prophecy at work, or people being delivered from demons and experiencing authentic freedom in their lives after years of emotional or even physical bondage. All that was wonderful to see and participate in, but the thing which gave it the most validity for me was to experience how God's presence tore down dividing walls that for so long caused division in the Body of Christ.

Catholics and Protestants, Pentecostals and Evangelicals who had become engulfed in the renewal, all fell in love. We fell in love with God in a much deeper way, but even more amazingly, we fell in love with each other. The Holy Spirit became a common denominator that overshadowed all of our differences. The unity we experienced was, for that moment, a preview of what could be and what should be.

Like all good things, the fervency of the renewal didn't last forever as we would have wished, but while it did, those who were present got a glimpse both of eternity and how, at least in part, the last days' church might one day look.

Spirit-filled Evangelicalism

In the midst of the Charismatic Renewal, a new leader arose who would change the complexion of Evangelicalism in our day. His named was John Wimber. Like so many of the revival leaders from the past, John was a talented musician and song writer with an amazing gift of communication. John could speak the language of normal people, converting complex theological ideas into easily understandable terms. In his earlier days, John had been a Las Vegas entertainer. He played the saxophone and piano, and wrote music for a popular band known as the Righteous Brothers. John had a powerful conversion from the Las Vegas lifestyle into Christianity, and like so many of us, he experienced a complete change of heart and a very real renewal of the mind. Almost immediately, he left his previous lifestyle and began a lifelong pursuit of Jesus. His testimony is more than I can mention here, but, in a matter of years, he became a church growth expert and worked on the staff at Fuller Theological Seminary. While consulting with a variety of denominational leaders across the country, John discovered something he wasn't expecting. He found that no matter the church's affiliation, the ones that had experienced the greatest growth had something in common. They all shared a similar theology of the Holy Spirit, and embraced the belief that people could experience God's presence the way the early church had in the Book of Acts. John knew all true Christian churches professed to be Trinitarian; that is to say, they all accepted a belief in the Father, Son, and Holy Spirit, but few Evangelical churches actually experienced the manifest presence of the Spirit. They all would say they believed in the Holy Spirt in Scripture, but in those days, only the Pentecostals would ask for the Spirit's presence to be manifest in their regular meetings. For the most part, it was only the Pentecostals who practiced speaking in tongues, prophesying, or praying for the sick as a regular part of their faith. Most Evangelicals saw this as emotional excessiveness. For them, the Baptism of the Holy Spirit and speaking in tongues, prophecy, and the other manifestations of the Holy Spirit ended with the Apostolic age.

John took issue with this and went about his ministry, proving that the Holy Spirit was still active in the church today. God honored John's sincere desire to make Christ's Spirit real for people. The Holy Spirit showed up in amazing ways, healing people and touching us so profoundly nobody could deny His presence.

God used John through the remainder of his life to bring this reality to many Evangelical churches around the world. For those of us who had been birthed out of the Jesus Movement, this new understanding was transformational. We learned that we could hear God for ourselves and even get marching orders for ways He had determined for us to serve Him.

For Nancy and me, it was initially to serve Him in the jungle on the border of Thailand and Burma. It was a radical time and promoted radical responses even in someone like me. We worked among a hill tribe people who had been undergoing ethnic cleansing for many years. Our efforts required our family to venture in and out of a war zone over the course of the next few years, something we would have never considered without an absolute conviction that God had called us and was with us. After our time in Burma, God clearly directed me to resign from my teaching position to become an assistant pastor in Southern California. That first assignment was a time of training and preparation, enabling us to embark on yet another incredible adventure. From Southern California, we moved our household to Idaho where we pioneered a new church in the capital city of Boise. Applying all I had learned concerning the heart of God, His word, the ups and downs of church history, and listening to His still small voice for direction, enabled our church to grow, thrive, and even transition to new leadership at my retirement. Without the prophetic voice of the Lord to direct us on our journey, I'm certain now that we would have made many wrong choices and taken more than one wrong turn on the road we traveled.

* * *

> I learned how being an Evangelical with head knowledge of God's plan alone would not be enough. The church would have to embrace the reality of an active Holy Spirit in order to have the strength, guidance, and prophetic foresight it would need in the turmoil of the days to come.
>
> * * *

All of these things we learned as participants in the Charismatic Renewal. Deep convictions were planted in my heart concerning God's desire and intentions for His church. It was then that I came to an understanding of how amazing true unity in the whole church can be. I learned how right and necessary it is in order for God's people to impact a suffering world. I learned how being an Evangelical with head knowledge of God's plan alone would not be enough. The church would have to embrace the reality of an active Holy Spirit in order to have the strength, guidance, and prophetic foresight it would need in the turmoil of the days to come. Not just for our personal survival, but to become a light in a darkening world.

Was American Evangelicalism losing its way?

By the mid '90s, something was changing in the Evangelical world. It was like a frog in the kettle; it was a slow, gradual shift, but for those who were living it, many sensed something was different. Our focus was changing and maybe not for the better. In an effort to explain, it will be necessary to recount a little more history.

Discovering "free love" had a high price

The '60s birthed some good things, but it also injected some things which became toxic to the emerging culture. The new morality popularized among the Hippie or Flower Child generation had at its epicenter the concept of free love. This loud proclamation openly announced the beginning of a sexual revolution that rapidly swept across our nation. The old credo, "If it feels good, do it," spread far beyond the Hippie movement. It was a statement which not only catered to man's appetite for sin, but relaxed the scruples of restraint in our generation.

Understanding the new attitudes that were rapidly emerging in the culture gives insight to the Supreme Court's landmark decision, Roe vs. Wade, legalizing abortion for the first time in American history. For some, Roe vs. Wade appeared to be a potential solution to the culture's newfound fear of overpopulation that plagued the early '70s. Few would admit it, but some who cared deeply about the earth's future destiny supported Roe vs. Wade because they saw it as a means of keeping "unwanted" people from adding to the growing concerns of overpopulation. Some secular environmental groups openly supported it, which angered Protestants and Catholics alike.

The issue of abortion awakened a sleeping giant. Evangelical Christians especially saw Row vs. Wade as a direct assault on the word of God, and a righteous anger arose, resulting in a loud cry of injustice on behalf of the unborn. Many non-believers had a difficult time understanding the anger. Because they had never experienced the "transformation of the mind" that occurs when someone gets in touch with the heart of God, they saw the Christian outcry as foolishness. "After all," they would say, "an embryo is not really a human life but merely undeveloped protoplasm." They pointed to the injustice of a woman who had been raped or a woman whose health was in jeopardy due to the birth process. They would also say that a teenage girl who became pregnant unintentionally, or the possibility of infant deformity, was justification enough to terminate pregnancy. For many, abortion seemed logical and even righteous, but for most Christians an abortion, for any reason, was unjustifiable. Because of their faith and an understanding that all life is sacred to God, and that every person is known to Him even in a mother's womb, abortion was nothing short of murder. For Christians, abortion violated the sanctity of life and would soon become a deal changer— a hill worth dying on.

This was the beginning of a war between conservative Christians and the liberal population that would both fight hard and passionately for a woman's right to choose the destiny of her unborn child. Roe vs. Wade sounded the first shot of a war, a war which had the potential of lasting until the second coming of Christ. Roe vs Wade motivated many powerful Evangelical leaders to turn to politics as a means of fighting this war.

Saved by grace, but no grace for the social Gospel

Pendulums always seem to have a way of swinging too far. When they do, they throw things out of balance. Sixty years before the battle which ignited over Roe vs. Wade, the Evangelical plumb bob went through a season of swinging to the left. Within the ranks of Evangelical leaders, a splinter group arose concerning issues of social injustice. The new movement emphasized a focus on Christian ethics as it related to the world's problems. Issues of social inequalities, such as extreme poverty, racial prejudice, environmental degradation, child labor, educational inequalities, and world violence were all focal points. Clergy across the country saw these things occurring in the culture and, with the best of intentions, wanted the church to engage in them. As the movement advanced, however, its extreme emphasis and theology became a concern to some Evangelical leaders who referred to it as the Social Gospel. The Social Gospel movement evolved into post-millennial thinking. Post-millennialists believed that Christ would not return until the church rose up and rid itself and the world of social injustice and evil. The movement had become fully humanistic, putting all the emphasis on mankind's good works.

This thinking created uproar among many Evangelical Christians who quoted Paul's words in Ephesians 2, *"But God, being rich in mercy, because of his great love with which he loved us, even though we were dead in transgressions, made us alive together with Christ—by grace you are saved!— and he raised us up with him and seated us with him in the heavenly realms in Christ Jesus, to demonstrate in the coming ages the surpassing wealth of his grace in kindness toward us in Christ Jesus. For by grace you are saved through faith, and this is not from yourselves, it is the gift of God; it is not from works, so that no one can boast"* (Ephesians 2:4-9, NET).

This became a foundational Scripture that would not only shut down the Social Gospel Movement, but would powerfully reignite Evangelicals into a season of new life. This passage said clearly that man can't earn his salvation. It is only by a combination of God's grace and man's faith that a person will receive eternal salvation, giving him access to heaven. Being a good person and doing good things, even godly things, would not get him to heaven. This restatement of what birthed Evangelicalism in the beginning, gave new life to the "born again" evangelistic movement. In the midst of it, men like Billy Graham rose up, experiencing tremendous favor and influence across the nation and around the world. It was a good time to be an Evangelical, not just in the days of Graham, but all the way to the end of the 20th century.

The problem was, in the strong reaction against the theology of the Social Gospel Movement, Evangelicals nearly always neglected to complete Paul's thought in Ephesians two. This emphasis that focused solely on grace and faith without good works may have caused the pendulum to swing too far. Again, revisiting the Ephesians passage, Paul finished his thought by saying: *"For we are his workmanship, having been created in Christ Jesus for good works that God prepared beforehand so we may do them"* (Ephesian 2:10, NET).

Yes, we are clearly saved by grace through faith. There is no earning our way into heaven, but Scripture is clear that with salvation comes responsibility. Jesus especially communicates to His believers that He has commissioned them to participate with Him, specifically in this very special period of human history between His first and second coming.

I say all this because the neglect of that one verse in Ephesians 2:10 will come home to roost in the 21st century, causing many young people to perceive traditional Evangelicalism as irrelevant in the times they live; a time when social injustice and extreme poverty would escalate.

The routinization of charisma — are we feeling it?

I've often used a statement I coined years ago, after reading the first chapters in the Book of Acts, that says, "Life begets life!" What I saw, especially in the second chapter of Acts, was a surge of spontaneous organic life spawned by a people who had freshly discovered how real God is. It was powerful and it was contagious. I realized then, the thing which must be present to keep any fresh move of God moving was a surge of life. There is excitement and fresh energy to believe in and even practice the impossible. The feelings I experienced in the early days of the Jesus Movement have in many ways sustained me even to this day. I remember the energy and thrill of seeing masses of my generation coming not only into a relationship with Christ, but with a willingness to serve Him in radical ways. There was life and that life drew others into it like a magnet.

* * *

The feelings I experienced in the early days of the Jesus Movement have in many ways sustained me even to this day.

* * *

For those of us who went out to plant new churches across the country, we knew how important those feelings of life in our communities would be. It was the best form of evangelism and church growth. It was the catalyst for momentum, and momentum was a crucial ingredient if we hoped to change our cities and impact our cultures. The kind of life we experienced was exhilarating and we never wanted it to go away. We lived on the crest of a wave which empowered our faith to believe God for anything, but like all waves, they eventually crest and begin to lose power. It's the normal cycle of life; it's just the way it is. The question is, can we carry on with faith and hope even if we aren't living on the crest? When the crest of the wave we are riding finally breaks and begins its less dramatic run up on to the sands of the beach, how will we respond?

In movements of God, the power that drives the wave is the Holy Spirit. The danger is, as the wave runs its natural cycle and begins to break, many leaders are unable to accept it. The charisma that was so present during one season of life is often manifested in distinctly visible ways. What generally characterized the crest of the wave during one move of God may not be as present in its aftermath. An example might be the manifestations of the Spirit, which so characterized both the Pentecostal movement in the early 1900s and later the Charismatic renewal. I wasn't there in the early days of Pentecostalism, but I was there during the Charismatic Renewal and I can testify that the manifestations of falling under the Spirit and times of spontaneous song and speaking in tongues were not made up. They were, in fact, very Spirit-inspired responses, but I also will testify that many, in their desperation of not losing what they had first experienced, continued to practice those manifestations when it was clearly not God doing it. In fact, these things became routine in many services and led to what has been referred to as the "routinization of charisma."

This also happened among Evangelicals. In the '70s and '80s, one of the most effective methods of evangelism took place when churches hosted Christian musicians who performed music and preached salvation messages in the context of concerts. God was in a season of using Christian bands to bring people to Himself. Week after week, churches would sponsor Christian musicians to do concerts in their facilities (mostly gymnasiums or warehouses) for the purpose of having the opportunity to share the Gospel. Literally thousands came to the Lord in these events. This method of evangelism became the norm until sometime in the '80s when the crowds dwindled down to primarily Christian audiences who had long ago given their lives to the Lord. The season was over, the crest of the wave had broken, and yet we kept doing it for at least ten more years, wondering what we were doing wrong. We had fallen into the trap of routinizing charisma. God had moved on to meet the culture in a fresh new way, but most of us failed to recognize it.

Not recognizing the routinization of charisma results in status quo and stagnated church life. Church loses its organic spontaneity, becoming regimented and ultimately, unappealing to outsiders. The life that birthed it is lost and people begin drifting to other expressions of Christianity or even back into their old secular ways. The only antidote to this slow-death process is leadership with prophetic insight. This is not only true of leaders, but of the congregations they lead. They, too, must see it and recognize the differences between good ideas and God-given direction. If there is ever to be a spiritual awakening in the 21st century, this truth must be heeded.

The rise of the para-church: Filling the gap

In 1960, a young man named Loren Cunningham had a vision while traveling in the Bahamas. In his vision, he saw waves breaking over the earth. Looking closer, he realized the waves were not made of water, but of young people, from all over the world, taking the message of Jesus on to the shores of every continent. The Lord told him that these young people would come from every nation and every Christian denomination to create a worldwide movement. Using the visionary statement, "Knowing God and making Him known," Loren and his wife, Darlene, began one of the most powerful para-church movements the world has ever known. Today, Youth with a Mission (more commonly known as YWAM) has 15,000 full-time volunteers working on established bases in 180 countries. This powerful team trains upward of 25,000 short-term missionaries every year.

YWAM came on to the Christian scene at a divine moment in church history. Although it was established in the early '60s, it was in full operation just in time to embrace thousands of young people who had been saved during the Jesus Movement revival. As only God could, His timing was perfect to provide an opportunity for intense discipleship and a means to serve Him in adventurous ways for thousands of young people who desired more than their local churches could offer.

YWAM provided a model for other emerging leaders to follow. Para-church ministries began to spring up across the country. Some focused-on discipleship and outreach opportunities, such as Last Days Ministries, founded by Keith and Melody Green, while others were established to do work the local churches neglected. Some focused on environmental degradation and others on issues of injustice, such as human trafficking. Some were formed for the sake of feeding the world's hungry, while others established schools or provided medical aid.

Some of the most visionary leaders who came out of the Jesus Movement could not find a place to exercise their passions within the local churches. Often these new leaders, sometimes more anointed and gifted than the local church leadership, became an annoyance to the churches they attended. Especially when it came to issues of social justice and the environment, they sometimes experienced flat out rejection, which forced them to leave and establish their own ministries. While Evangelicalism, in general, increasingly pushed back on issues of justice and the environment, well-meaning Christians took it upon themselves to pursue the things they believed were important to God. As a result, Evangelical churches not only lost gifted leaders, but the passions they championed.

* * *

The church will become a major agency of justice and compassion on the earth and that will be magnetic to the unchurched world.

* * *

When the end times' church finally arises, these lost passions will be re-embraced by the local church and become a driving force for a fresh new work of God. The church will become a major agency of justice and compassion on the earth and that will be magnetic to the unchurched world.

Era of Christian consumerism and
the birth of the church growth movement

As the fervor of the Jesus Movement began to subside, many churches began looking for new expressions of ministry for the people who had long ago given their lives to Christ but still had deep-felt needs. In some ways, the church was becoming a smorgasbord of diverse ministry in order to meet the outcry. There was something for everyone and excellence became a priority. Some have referred to it as the age of consumeristic Christianity.

Before the Jesus Movement revival began building momentum across America, a church with a Sunday attendance of two or three hundred was considered a large church. The average size of a local church was somewhere in the neighborhood of seventy-five people, but because the new models of doing church were working, churches started to grow.

I was the pastor of a church that grew to two thousand plus people on a twenty-five-acre campus in the heart of Boise, Idaho. Nancy and I founded and then pastored the Boise Vineyard for twenty-five years. By megachurch standards, it was on the lower end of the attendance scale, but it was, by definition, a megachurch all the same. It was a far cry from the seventy-five person average churches of the '60s and '70s. By the year 2000, megachurches were everywhere across America. After the Charismatic renewal and a season of, what might be referred to as the church conference era, people discovered they loved the energy and excitement of larger gatherings. Worship seemed more dynamic when hundreds of people sang together in large auditoriums. Because congregations were larger, the financial resources for ministry were greater. We could do more because we could afford larger professional staffs to head up a diversity of ministries. With more people, we could mobilize large workforces of lay people, who in turn, could more effectively reach their communities and cities. We had entire facilities to serve the poor with food, medicine, clothing, and other services. We had teams to reach into the prisons and others to provide recovery ministry for the addicted. We had gymnasiums, state-of-the-art children and youth facilities, facilities for artists, and others for people focused on global missions. The introduction of the megachurch was not all bad, by any means.

Coming from the perspective of a leader who was fully engaged in the church growth movement, I can speak to both its advantages and disadvantages. First off, I'd say growing megachurches served the Body of Christ well for a season. They were right for their time; a time that I believe has not yet passed. The megachurch met a culture that believed and may still believe, that bigger is better, more dynamic, and can reach further.

On the down side, however, the church-growth era created a new definition of success for young emerging pastors to strive for; a definition that was neither biblical nor realistic. Most megachurches were built around charismatic personalities who could draw large assemblies and had the gifting to organize their growing churches using higher level business models. For these reasons, retiring megachurch leaders are now finding it difficult to pass their life work on to an emerging generation. This phenomenon is reality for three reasons:

• First, many of the Millennial generation do not have the life experience or management skills needed to lead large infrastructures.
• Second, they may lack the charisma to cast compelling vison.
• Third, and most significantly, they lack the desire or motivation to carry on what they perceive as being "corporate church."

Preaching the gospel was and always will be the most important thing, but building a large church took a whole new level of leadership gifting. The pressure to attract larger numbers of people often distorted a leader's motivation and energy focus. Forgetting that authentic discipleship was a higher priority to God than gathering large crowds, leaders often fell into the trap of catering to consumerism. This meant more energy would be put into things like state-of-the- art sound systems, high-class facilities, and professional videography, rather than meeting the needs of the poor and bringing people to maturity in Christ.

Another negative issue of the megachurch was its conduciveness for people to hide in a crowd and remain a spectator. Those who had the motivation and fortitude to engage thrived, but those who suffered with a sense of inferiority often were overlooked and left behind. Some would say the megachurch lacked intimacy and relationship even when it could be found in small groups and specialty ministries.

I, for one, believe in the effectiveness of the megachurch in today's world, but also realize that if harder times come to America, things might well change. For example, during the 1970s, America experienced an energy shortage which created hour-long lines at the gas pumps. I remember how that crisis, although short lived, caused an overnight shift in the way people thought about commuting long distances, especially to things like church services. Today, people think nothing of passing a dozen local churches as they commute across an entire city to attend a more popular megachurch. A more extreme and possibly a less likely example might be persecution. If real persecution erupts as the Bible says it someday will, the church will be motivated to become less visible. In this case, larger churches would have great difficulty reorganizing and adapting to meet the needs of their people. If Christianity becomes a threat to the culture, many nominal Christians would fall away, leaving only those willing to put their lives on the line to foot the bill to support expensive facilities. If there was an economic crisis, not like the recession of 2008 but a real depression, large churches with big debt loads would be the first to suffer. Times like these are not unrealistic to consider in an era of extreme political unrest and uncertainty. Churches that are focused on paying the bills will be too distracted to put their energies and resources into world evangelism, especially considering that most of this work will be done among the extremely poor.

The Prophetic Voices: Will
we know them when we hear them?

During the Charismatic Renewal, many Spirit-filled Evangelical ministries witnessed a season of prophetic voices. Some of these voices were impressively accurate. They were often highly charismatic speakers who had the ability to draw large Christian audiences. They spoke with great authority and had supernatural insight into people's personal lives without having previous knowledge of them. By revealing these things, people became awestruck, and then accepted the exhortations and encouragements that followed. Many of these prophetic people had very real gifting, but these are not the prophetic voices I'm speaking of here.

Before a major new move of God, there are often prophetic voices that herald it. They don't cause it, but they see it coming. Those are the voices that count and the ones we want to recognize when we hear them. The experiences we had in the '80s and '90s are important to mention because they gave us an awareness of what to listen for. They also reminded us not to become too overly mesmerized by those who happened to have a gift.

In the Old Testament, most of the prophets were not impressive, they did not draw large crowds, and they were often the most unexpected people to carry the word of the Lord. Most of them were looked upon as eccentric, and many were rejected altogether. This worries me, because it shows how easy it would be to miss them and the messages they deliver. How will we know?

Unfortunately, we generally will only know after years pass and we see the warnings they brought us becoming reality. That's a bummer! On the other hand, however, if we ourselves are sensitive to the Spirit and are earnestly seeking God for future truth, when something is said or written that rings true, often our spirits will bear witness to it. What we have to be careful of is that these voices often don't come from the pulpit. In fact, these voices can be from any expression of the Christian faith—Catholic, Protestant, or even from someone outside the faith. The important thing is that we learn to discern these voices, especially during times when there is excessive deception in the culture. As we prepare for the days ahead, we must desire more than anything that God would grant us a new level of spiritual discernment. This thought will be essential as we move on in our journey of learning to live in the last days. We will focus on the words of Paul in 2 Corinthians 11 where he said, *"But I am afraid that just as the serpent deceived Eve by his treachery, your minds may be led astray from a sincere and pure devotion to Christ"* (NET).

The Prosperity Doctrine: Catering to the "great American dream" of personal wealth, health, and security

Almost every form of Christian heresy is based on some level of biblical truth, but strays from authenticity when it caters to the self-centered nature of man. The Prosperity Doctrine, otherwise known as "Name it and Claim it" Christianity, became popular and gained rapid momentum in the 1990s. It was primarily promoted by televangelists who discovered they could accumulate great wealth through preaching this doctrine. They believed being poor was a result of a person's sin and that God's intention was for everyone to experience financial prosperity. They professed that all of these blessings would come through positive confession, visualization, and generous donations to religious causes.

* * *

Almost every form of
Christian heresy is
based on some level
of biblical truth,
but strays from
authenticity when
it caters to the
self-centered
nature of man.

* * *

God appears to use everything to prepare His people for His plans and purposes, even the preaching of heresy for personal gain. It always surprised me how people who had some sense of the Bible could buy into something that seemed so contrary to the heart of God. For many of us leading churches in those days, we found ourselves repulsed by how many television evangelists were obviously taking advantage of gullible, needy people. We were also outraged that these charlatans were turning so many unchurched people, the very people we were trying to share God's love with, away from Christianity. The culture began mistrusting Evangelicals all the more. It became uncomfortable for pastors to tell people in secular circles what we did for a living. When it came out, we often became suspect, losing the credibility and respect pastors once enjoyed. It was uncomfortable, but looking at in retrospect, I can now appreciate what God was doing.

For the first time, we felt a twinge of what it was like to be unpopular and even, to a degree, persecuted for our convictions. This did two things: one, it forced us to look for new approaches to reach the broken world, and second, it forced the pendulum to swing the opposite direction into total honesty, transparency, and authenticity. For us, there could be no lack of integrity; our credibility was fully on the line and our effectiveness depended on it. We were under the magnifying glass of a world that mistrusted our words and actions. This was a good thing, because the new generation soon to be taking our place of leadership would observe and hopefully imitate this kind of character. It could be that this new generation leads the end times' church. For them, authenticity and sincerity will be absolutely essential.

A culture desperate for interpersonal healing

Seventy years ago, the psychologist Abraham Maslow produced a concept he referred to as the pyramid, or hierarchy, of human needs. At the base of his five- tiered pyramid is a foundation stone called Basic needs. This stone is the largest and the foundation for all the others. Basic needs are defined as air, water, and food, in that order. The second stone is Safety. This stone represents the human need to feel physically and emotionally secure. The third is Love: the need for intimacy, family, and friends. The fourth is Self-esteem: the need to feel significant, to have respect, to be wanted and needed. The final stone is Self-actualization: the need to feel fulfilled, to discover one's purpose in life.

Maslow's theory states that these needs come in a particular order. As each level of need is satisfied, the desire to fulfil the next level kicks in. In other words, if a person is without air, he is only motivated to get a breath, not satisfy his thirst. If he is without water, he cares little about hunger. Only when his basic needs are met is he motivated to satisfy the next tier of the pyramid, which is personal safety, and so on.

For the most part, Americans at the end of the 20th century worried little about basic and safety needs. There was little motivation to be concerned about breathable air, drinkable water, or nutritional food. For the most part, things were pretty secure which motivated the culture to move to the upper tiers of Maslow's pyramid: love, self-esteem, and self-actualization. Many turned to the church for help.

Maslow's hierarchy of needs
1. Basic — air, water, food
2. Safety — feeling secure
3. Love — Intimacy, family, friends
4. Self-esteem — significance, respect, being wanted and needed
5. Self-actualization — fulfillment, personal development, fulfilling life's purpose

As a result, the culture during the '80s and '90s became introspective and self-focused, resulting in many church ministries emphasizing personal emotional healing. The bestselling Christian publications of the day, other than the Bible itself, were books focusing on self-help. People seemed driven to get relief from their broken pasts and the memories that robbed their joy. Many of their needs were legitimate, especially considering the dysfunction that came out of the '60s. As I said before, our generation was finding out that "free love" wasn't free. We also found out that responding to a belief system which endorsed doing whatever felt good at the moment, no matter the cost to others, created a really broken society.

By the end of the '80s, the divorce rate in the church was no different than in the secular world. We had become a fatherless society, and both feelings of rejection and reactions of rebellion became the norm. We were a society desperately searching for significance, and frequently found ourselves looking for it in all the wrong places. In an effort to meet the need and attract people to our tables, we built church ministries that catered to the pain. Somehow, conventional church teaching wasn't enough for many people, which motivated them to search out more mystical types of ministry in the hopes of receiving healing and freedom. This changed the complexion of many Evangelical churches; they saw themselves become more like hospitals than agencies of cultural change. Again, at least in part, Evangelicalism lost focus on its outward commission to go into the world with the gospel of God's Kingdom, making disciples.

It is a sad truth, but truth all the same, that man's motivation to pursue God's intervention happens best in times of trial and suffering. The suffering of the '80s and '90s was primarily emotional, not physical. Our basic needs were being met and we felt enough physical security because we lived in the land of the free. Things were good, but as the old adage goes, "Where there is no pain, there is no gain." What the church would need, if there was to be another major spiritual awakening, was a little pain, something the 21st century would soon provide.

The Moral Majority: A game-changer for Evangelicals

Do you recall how revivals in the past (the examples we used were the Protestant Reformation and the Great Awakening) always came out of a season where the Church had become entangled with the political system of their day? If you go back further, the same thing was true in the days of Jesus and the Book of Acts. The Jews who first followed Jesus expected Him to become a political king rather than a spiritual one. They didn't get it. Jesus told His followers to *"Give to Caesar the things that are Caesar's, and to God the things that are God's"* (Mark 12:17, NET). He exhorted His followers to separate their activities as believers from the secular thinking of Rome. In other words, to separate church and state.

In 1979, a group of high-profile Christian leaders led by a Baptist pastor named Jerry Falwell, gathered to discuss how they might mobilize American Evangelical believers across the country in order to influence the American political system. They were angry at what they perceived to be rapid moral decay across the nation. They were very angry about the Supreme Court's decision to legalize abortion and concluded the only way they could control our changing culture was through the vehicle of politics. The efforts of these men, as they linked arms with another conservative group known as the Religious Right, began influencing Evangelical Christians, Catholics, Mormons, and Jews across the country. Together, they advanced socially conservative positions on issues such as school prayer, intelligent design, embryonic stem cell research, homosexuality, abortion, and pornography. Their efforts swept the nation throughout the '80s and '90s, and changed the complexion of Evangelicalism. Christians were perceived more as right-wing Republicans than sincere promoters of the Kingdom of God. The line between church and state became blurred while the line between liberals and conservatives grew into a major dividing wall.

Two camps and one nation divided

By the mid-nineties, two camps had been clearly established and the majority of Evangelical Christians chose to pitch their tents in the conservative camp. When people take sides after drawing lines in the sand, loyalty arises among them. As they begin to identify and clarify the ideologies that unite them, they soon become defensive against any who would challenge their convictions. When the other side questions, challenges, or ridicules those beliefs, they then are quickly perceived as enemies. We may all be Americans, but now one side or the other redefines themselves as "true Americans." As things progressed in the final years of the 20th century, America evolved into what became referred to as "one nation divided."

The trouble with having two defined camps is that critical issues become polarizing rather than points of discussion. Some of these issues, however, are so critical to the welfare of all, they should be embracd by everyone rather than pigeonholed into one camp or the other. Two good examples are the environment and social justice.

Evangelicals push environmentalism and social justice into the liberal camp

Creation care and social justice are two very clear biblical agendas. In Genesis 9, God established a covenant with His creation which became known as the "Noahic Covenant" or the "Covenant of the Rainbow." It was a covenant which commissioned all of His people to become stewards of creation.

For those who read their Bible and believe it, this should have been a no-brainer when the liberal / conservative lines were drawn, but the fact is, both environmental stewardship and issues of justice were rejected by conservatives and became liberal agendas. Some might ask, how were they hijacked? The answer is simple: liberals didn't hijack these biblical responsibilities, they took them on because conservatives had turned their backs on them.

Reviewing the ground we've already covered, let's go back to the Jesus Movement and recall what was going on in the minds of these young, new, Christian believers. Two huge things happened: One, we were afraid because we saw our world entering a state of environmental crisis due to overpopulation and human entitlement. The problem seemed too big and too impossible to fix. When the Jesus Movement impacted our generation, it brought an answer and some hope to our fears; the answer was eschatology. The extreme focus on this biblical truth caused us to overlook the biblical responsibility of creation care. As our Bible teachers and preachers told us, the environment didn't really matter because they said, "It's all going to burn anyway." Those who hadn't come to Christ wrote off this cavalier attitude as being illogical nonsense. They dismissed the church as being irrelevant and continued their concern for the future welfare of the earth and its impact on humanity. They saw this as an issue of social justice because if the earth became unsustainable, it would cause extreme human suffering.

The second issue that caused conservative Christians to push back on the environment was the liberal victory of Roe vs. Wade and the legalization of abortion. If you recall our previous conversation, secular environmental groups backed Row vs. Wade as a possible means of controlling overpopulation. As a result, they were pushed by Evangelicals into the "enemy" camp of liberalism.

Concerning social justice issues in general, there were two other reasons these issues were neglected by numerous Evangelicals. The first reason was their push back on the social gospel from the early 1900s which still remained in the Evangelical DNA. The second reason was due to popular conservative voices which began speaking into the right-wing camp. Many of these conservative personalities began equating social justice with socialism. One such radio personality exhorted his listeners to leave the church they were attending if the pastor even mentioned the words "social justice."

Angry voices and the redefining of Evangelicalism

Starting sometime in the 1980s, conservative talk radio and television commentators became the voices for the far right. Because many Evangelicals identified with the values proclaimed by these rising celebrities, they saw them as voices of truth. Some of these popular personalities professed to be people of faith and although many of the things they said supported Christian values, their anger, arrogance, and authoritarian rhetoric did not communicate the character of Jesus.

As their voices became more popular throughout Christian culture, many well-meaning pastors became fearful to say anything negative about them. In many ways, their voices overpowered the words of sincere Christian leaders who were attempting to instill the nature of Christ in their people. It became a conflict so discordant that many leaders decided to join them rather than fight, sometimes even to the point of supporting political candidates and directing voter choices.

Feeling intimidated, pastors began avoiding biblical issues altogether, such as the case with creation care. They steered clear from issues of social injustice, causing their congregations to neglect God's many mandates to care for broken humanity. Evangelicalism was becoming redefined, especially to the unchurched world. To many outside the church, the word "Evangelical" became a nasty word as it was perceived to be a controlling, political organization rather than a lover of neighbors. We, as Christians, began losing credibility and attractiveness to those we were called to reach. Evangelicalism was no longer equated with Christ-like evangelism but rather, a right-wing political agenda.

Y2K: A false alarm but an alarm all the same

In 1999, the developed world had a momentary scare. Just before the turn of the new century, computer programmers sounded an alarm. They expressed a concern for what they thought would be a major worldwide computer glitch. Computers up until that time had represented the year's four-digit date with only the last two digits. Some said that if computers weren't corrected when the year 2000 (hence the acronym Y2K) came, the date would be misinterpreted as being the year 1900. This simple mistake would make computers everywhere go haywire, simultaneously shut down, causing catastrophic global crises. It was believed by many that as computer systems crashed, the world would technologically shut down, impacting global communication, transportation, government, electrical grids, water delivery systems, and the means for food distribution.

It may sound crazy now, but having been there it did raise genuine concern. People were scared, not knowing exactly what they should do. For the first time, we became aware of how completely dependent we were on computer systems, and how vulnerable we had become in such a short time. The threat of a disaster of this magnitude also made us realize how unprepared we were for any kind of catastrophic disaster. If Y2K or any other crises of its magnitude occurred, a vast majority of the population would be starving within days as grocery shelves emptied. Many ignored the threat altogether, believing that things would always carry on in America and nothing would ever change. In fact, it did turn out to be a false alarm, but it was for many an alarm all the same. I know it was for me.

Having lived on the old family homestead the first twenty years of our marriage taught our family a lot about preparation and self-sufficiency. We had lived the first fifteen of those years without electricity, and relied on spring water piped down the mountain for our water. I cut firewood to keep us warm in the winter and to fuel the kitchen cook stove. We had planted both an orchard and kitchen garden to provide our family with fruits and vegetables, and raised and hunted animals for meat. I can remember when we were snowed in for weeks at a time and never missed a meal. We ate Nancy's canned goods and butchered an occasional chicken. We didn't miss the power being out because we had our own electrical generator. We were not only set up to take care of ourselves, but were in a position to help our neighbors. Later, after moving our family to Idaho and planting a new church in Boise, we adapted to city life with all of its amenities. Y2K was a reminder of how vulnerable to crisis we had become.

As Y2K approached, I started to think about the church. It, too, was vulnerable to crisis or calamity of any kind. I wasn't thinking about the last days then, but our unpreparedness made me think how helpless we would be if Y2K was real or any other kind of catastrophe struck our city. I didn't just want to be in a position to care for our people, but to be a resource for the city. That year we constructed a huge warehouse, calling it the Barnabas Center, and stocked it with non-perishable foods. We contacted the local Red Cross and offered our facility as a crisis center, and had them train our staff to run it. If disaster struck, I wanted the church to be a helpful blessing to our community rather than being helplessly panicked like everyone else.

People mocked us as being eccentric, but later, after the threat of Y2K had passed, our preparation gave us one of the best food pantries in the city. Our people had planted a two-acre vegetable garden that supplied the community with 30,000 pounds of organic vegetables every year. Members of our congregation, with health care training, set up a wing of the Barnabas Center as a free medical clinic. Nothing was lost, but much was gained. Y2K had become a great blessing to the life of the church. It also served as a lesson for many as to what a last days' church might look like when hard times and calamity threatened the security and comfort of American Christians.

Y2K warned us of just how dependent we had become on technology. In those days, we couldn't fathom the vulnerability we would one day experience with computer identify fraud, cybersecurity, and cyberterrorism. We also didn't know that in a matter of a few years, nearly every American would carry a computer on their person for daily life assistance. It would be used twenty-four hours a day for such things as communication, banking and accounting needs, GPS guidance, buying and selling, and even entertainment. Every citizen would soon become connected to satellite tracking and literally be woven into an interconnected global network. To most, it sounded like science fiction fantasy, but in a matter of fifteen years it became reality. Ignoring the warning of Y2K, we became assimilated without even caring. Our blissfulness may one day come back to bite us. Our total dependence on computers is a growing threat and a crack in the foundation of America's security.

Enters "The Age of Information" and a time of Parenthesis

In the mid-1980s, I read a book by a man named David McKenna called *Mega Truth — The Church in the Age of Information*. Concerning the type of prophecy which predicts things God is doing in preparation for a future event, McKenna's book may be the most prophetic thing I've ever read. I felt his writing to be profound when I read it in 1986, but now, reflecting back on the things McKenna wrote 30 years ago, I am astonished at his insights and the accuracy of his projections.

In 1986, few church leaders even owned a computer. Email was just coming on line, the worldwide internet was still in the future, and social media was a complete unknown. I remember moving to Boise to plant the Vineyard Christian Fellowship in 1989. Our family was accompanied by twelve other families and a few single people who felt called to join us. One of our single guys named Ruben was a very forward-looking, progressive guy. Ruben saw the necessity of computers for the future of the church. I was still writing sermons on an electric typewriter at the time and couldn't see it. Ignoring my thinking, Ruben brought along a used computer from our previous church for its word processor capabilities. Honestly, that computer looked like something that came from Toys R Us, but it served us well for the first year of our church plant. It's hard to believe, but that was less than 30 years ago.

McKenna shared in his book that our culture was starting to shift from the Industrial Revolution into the Age of Information. He shared that historically, every time a culture goes through a major transition of eras, it experiences what he called "Cultural Disjuncture." Cultural disjuncture speaks of a deep sense of unrest, despair, and hopelessness that often occurs in the undercurrents of a society during a state of transition. McKenna calls this phase of transition from era-to-era a time of "Parenthesis," and explains that every major move of God occurs during such a time. Both the Reformation of Luther's day and the Great Awakening of Wesley's day were birthed at such a time.

McKenna projected that as we move into this new era, we will begin to experience cultural disjuncture, even as we did in a much smaller way during the '60s. If McKenna is right, and history says he is, then America is ripe for a major spiritual awakening. The Jesus Movement was a blip on the radar, comparatively. It was a small, local (primarily Southern California) revival, but far from the awakening McKenna believes could occur.

He shared that every revival and spiritual awakening starts among a demographic he called "New Lights." The New Lights are often found on college and university campuses. They are an emerging adult generation, seeking truth for their future, and are willing to sacrifice everything to obtain it. They are radical and possess the resolve and idealism to engage in revolutions. The "New Lights" in the 21st century may well be the Millennial generation, who will be entering their college and young adult years in the 2020s.

All the events I have shared so far are things God has divinely allowed and put into place to prepare His church for such a time as now. We are presently starting to experience and observe in our nation and around the world the full manifestation of cultural disjuncture. The question will be as McKenna had stated so many years before — will the "new lights" rise to the occasion? I believe there is much work to be done.

Part II

WHAT IS

A World Unraveling

9-11: A new reality threatens the American dream

My wife Nancy is Irish. Not just Irish, but Irish Catholic. Both her mother and father's side of the family had come to America as immigrants just a couple of generations before. Growing up, the two most revered days of the year for her family were Christmas Day and Saint Patrick's Day. From the day I married her I wanted to take her to Ireland, but raising a growing family on a teacher or minister's salary made saving vacation money a challenge. It wasn't until our thirty-first wedding anniversary in August of 2001 that things came together to make the trip happen.

We had been asked to sit on the National Vineyard Church executive board which met in different parts of the country for its annual meetings. In 2001, it was to meet on the coast of Maine on September 11th. The timing was perfect for us because it provided us with nine days to drive around Southern Ireland before returning to the States for our meetings. We booked our tickets from Boise to Dublin via Logan airport in Boston.

Returning to the States, we landed at Logan International Airport on the evening of September 10th. We were flying on United Airlines. I hate long lines and crowded spaces, especially in roped-off corridors like the ones experienced at customs, and was relieved to see officers casually waving people through without giving luggage a second look. It was the easiest re-entry into the United States we'd ever experienced and I commented on it to Nancy. "Wow," I laughed. "That was sure painless." "Too painless," Nancy responded. "Those guys didn't even look at us, they were so caught up in their own conversation with each other." It was a quick interaction, but one we would recall with terror the next day.

We drove up to Maine that evening and checked into our hotel room, hoping for a decent night's sleep in preparation for the meetings scheduled to start the next morning. In the morning, I was getting things together in the hotel room, readying myself to head for the conference room. Nancy was still brushing her teeth, and with a few minutes to kill, I turned on the morning news station just in time to see fire coming out one of the 110-story twin towers of the World Trade Center. The news commentator was alarmed, but uncertain what was going on. She said it had been reported that a plane had accidentally crashed into the tower. Like so many people across the country, I watched in unbelief on live TV as the second jet hit the second tower. This was clearly not an accident, but a purposeful attack.

Nancy and I rushed to the conference room where we joined the rest of our colleagues, and together witnessed the remaining events of what later became known as 9-11. In a matter of an hour and forty-two minutes, four commercial jets crashed, killing 2,996 innocent people and injuring 6,000 others.

Nineteen Islamic terrorists from Al-Qaeda had hijacked four large U.S. air carriers bound from two northeastern airports to Los Angeles, fully loaded with people and jet fuel. The attack had been strategically planned for many months and was executed with clockwork perfection.

For Nancy and me, the reality of 9-11 was a wake-up call. It reminded us of how fragile and precious life is; it reminded us of our mortality. A sobering thought was that we were scheduled to fly out two days later from the same airport on the same transcontinental airline chosen by the hijackers. Logan Airport was shut down for six weeks following the attack, which left us stranded at a time when we desperately wanted to be with our children and our church family. We realized then, if we were to live through the next era of time victoriously, we would not only need to be prepared emotionally and physically, but even more so, spiritually. I recalled Peter's words as he spoke of the final days in 2 Peter 3, where he warned us to be on our guard so we would not be carried away by the errors of others and lose our own secure footing. The new millennium would be a time of pressing more deeply into God. For me, it would be a time to hear His voice and not be influenced by the loud humanistic voices of fearful people. 9-11 was a time to refocus and reprioritize.

America was shaken to the core. The reality of just how vulnerable we had become was beyond our belief. From that point on, everything would change for a people who hadn't experienced a foreign enemy attack on their soil since the War of 1812. It was a shock to American culture, shaking a sense of security we had taken for granted and stimulating a new era of fear and outrage. The new millennium had arrived and would be accompanied with pain and discomfort.

The era of the "Teens": The '60s on steroids

Two weeks after the Trump inauguration, on a Charlie Rose NBC interview, Frank Luntz, a Republican strategist, was asked about his take on the escalating riots and protests happening since the start of Trump's presidency. Specifically, Charlie asked about the destructive rioting that broke out on the University of California Berkeley campus. Luntz responded by saying he felt America was becoming unraveled, adding that he prayed we weren't returning to 1968. His comment caused me to reflect on the events that brought such distinctiveness to the '60s and early '70s. I compare the magnitude of those signs of cultural disjuncture with our present day — a time I will refer to as the "era of the teens." The 1920s was later referred to as the "roaring twenties" and the 1960s simply as the '60s because they both reflected seasons of major cultural change. I believe 2010 through 2020 (or the "Teens") will also one day be recognized as extraordinary. This fact is significant in our discussion on spiritual awakening. As we have seen already, awakenings have always emerged from the ashes and rubble of cultural shaking.

Causes of cultural disjuncture during eras of American Culture

1960s	2000 — Teens
Mistrust in the political system	America is politically divided in anger
A war against communism (Vietnam)	A global war against terrorism
Political protests by young radicals	Protests across all generations
Civil rights for Black Americans	Black Lives Matter movement builds new momentum
Heterosexual revolution	Homosexual revolution
Fear of global environmental decline	International fear concerning climate change
Fear of projected population growth	Reality of a non-sustainable world
Women's liberation movement birthed	6-8 million women march globally
Drug culture birthed	Opioid epidemic sweeps America

My thesis is simply this: the 2000-teens are the 1960s on steroids. Having personally experienced the '60s, I can attest to the fact that what we are daily experiencing as we enter 2017 far overshadows any events of the '60s in magnitude. During the '60s, we feared the uncertainty of a distant future; today, we are beginning to live in the manifestation of that future. Our country and the world is, in fact, in serious trouble!

In the 1960s, the Boomer generation mistrusted political leaders because of two major events, the Vietnam War and Watergate. In 2016, a large portion of the American culture is disillusioned not only with the executive branch of government, but the House and Senate as well. Politics became a point of great concern and negativity with all generations, but especially among the Millennials. Polls showed that in the 2016 election, much of the nation voted for what they considered to be the lesser of two evils. The sad news is, if you vote for the lesser of evils, in the final analysis the winner will still be perceived as evil.

In the 1960s, the Boomer generation (college age at the time) rose in anger against every kind of social injustice—civil rights for Black Americans, women's rights, and the impact of environmental degradation on plants, animals, and humans. They marched in anger by the thousands. Today, protests against a political leader's ideology do not only occur on American university campuses, but in the streets of hundreds of cities and towns and in nations around the world. Protesters are not numbered in the thousands but the millions. Contradictorily to their passionate past, Boomers made up the majority of Trump supporters in 2016, desiring security and government protection above the idealistic issues they so vigorously stood for in the '60s.

In the 1960s, a sexual revolution began challenging the traditional norm of "saving" yourself for a monogamous relationship. The '60s revolution formulated new values for heterosexual relationships. In the 20-teens, a new sexual revolution is raging, this time for homosexual freedoms: for gay rights, same-sex marriage, and bisexual acceptance. Times have definitely changed in these regards.

The fears so many of us felt in the '60s concerning future environmental decline, fears that later many dismissed as the agenda of radical liberals, are now coming back to bite us. Ice caps are melting, sea levels are rising, and low land cities are experiencing devastating flooding. Skeptics are quickly becoming believers, but are still pushing back on the kinds of change needed to make a difference. Weather is taking a toll on our nation, but fossil fuel is still the king. Even as warnings are being shouted from the roof tops, many understand that unless there is total global reformation, whatever we do may be too late. It is a message of doom that is penetrating the souls of a generation, instilling low-grade depression and hopelessness, as they witness government leaders bickering over positions of power while ignoring global threats against humanity.

I think there were prophetic voices coming from the music of the '60s, voices of prophets we didn't recognize at the time. For sure, Dylan was in touch with something when he proclaimed "The Times They Are A-Changin'," but he may have not realized that they would change more in the season of the 2000-teens than they ever would in the era he wrote his poetry. And, at that time, I'm not sure how prophetic we could have known his words were when he sang about the waters rising. There hasn't been any musical lyrics I know of written since that so clearly describes the devastation of climate change.

Simon and Garfunkel may have seen it, too, when they sang, "Bridge over Troubled Waters" in 1970. They sang about someone being a comforter in times when darkness comes, when pain is everywhere, when our lives feel like they are full of troubled waters. This song spoke of someone, a friend and a comforter, who would lay down his/her life like a bridge to cover over it all. What Simon and Garfunkel may not have known was that the comfort they spoke of in bringing relief from pain and being light where there is darkness would be Christ Himself. He would be the friend and only He could lay himself down like a bridge when everything else is turning to ruin. When that happens, when people come to realize how much they are in need of that bridge, then everything will change. Then, and only then, there will be the motivation for people

> *** It is a message of doom that is penetrating the souls of a generation, instilling low-grade depression and hopelessness, as they witness government leaders bickering over positions of power while ignoring global threats against humanity. ***

to look to God for help. At such a time, there is the potential for a spiritual awakening capable of turning ashes to beauty and hope where there is only despair. Yes, it will change everything, but the ashes will surely come before the beauty; the troubled waters before man will see his need for a bridge.

Preparing the heart for a season of "troubled waters"

The power of suffering

I've never met anybody who really likes to suffer. I know I don't; I try to avoid it at all cost if I can. If anyone says they like to suffer, I'd say there's something wrong with them, but the fact is, suffering is a part of the human experience. No one I know is fully exempt, yet compared to the rest of the world, being born into middle class America definitely has its advantages. The average American finds it hard to believe that over fifty percent of the world's population lives in extreme poverty, subsisting on two dollars or less a day. Most Americans can't comprehend what that kind of suffering really feels like. In fact, many Americans feel entitled to the blessed life they've enjoyed and will do almost anything to protect it, even if it means compromising their belief system.

The thought of us not having three meals a day or being able to keep gasoline in our automobiles is inconceivable. We take for granted the clean water we drink and the security we have felt as a middle or upper class society for so many years. This isn't to say there hasn't been poverty and injustice among us, but even our poor have access to government and social programs that provide some relief. Things, however, are genuinely changing and as the millennium advances towards the year 2020, we are sensing the great American dream may not always be as wholesome and carefree as we thought. The days of "Leave it To Beaver" and "Happy Days" with the Fonz may be fading into a distant memory as things like violence and environmental crises begin to escalate.

In the '70s and '80s, pre-trib Christians were convinced they would escape the suffering of the last days' tribulation they saw in the Bible. If anyone in those days had a contrary view, pre-tribs would dismiss it as negative confession and sinful thinking. Funny, Jesus himself said, "*In the world you will have tribulation.*" But He also added, *"But take heart; I have over-come the world"* (John 16:33, ESV). Bad news and good news, but if we are going to have tribulation, we want Jesus with us when it happens!

You might have a hard time convincing the Christians that were eaten by lions in Rome, or the thousands upon thousands of martyrs who were executed for their faith under the rule of the Chinese Marxist Mao Tse Tung, that Christians are exempt from tribulation and suffering. Concerning the last days, however, Jesus did say that the suffering humanity would experience will be cut short. He said, *"For there will be greater anguish in those days than at any time since God created the world. And it will never be so great again. In fact, unless the Lord shortens that time of calamity, not a single person will survive. But for the sake of his chosen ones he has shortened those days"* (Mark 13: 19-20, NLT). All this to say, I don't think Christians are exempt from suffering, but I do believe God will use it for good. I hate to say it, but there is power in suffering.

The Apostle Paul said, *"We can rejoice, too, when we run into problems and trials, for we know that they help us develop endurance. And endurance develops strength of character, and character strengthens our confident hope of salvation. And this hope will not lead to disappointment. For we know how dearly God loves us, because he has given us the Holy Spirit to fill our hearts with his love"* (Romans 5:3-5, NET). In summary, suffering equals endurance, endurance equals strength of character, and strength of character equals hope. In short, suffering produces hope and hope will never disappoint us.

Not long ago I heard a CBS Christmas interview with Cardinal Timothy Dolan. He said hope has always been life's greatest question. Mankind has always wanted to know how to find it and hang on to it. He said hope may be in some ways more important to man than faith, explaining that people might lose faith for a time and get by, but if they lose hope they can't get out of bed in the morning. Without hope we become paralyzed and helpless.

When we suffer and turn to God we get to see Him work in magnificent ways. Remember the promise of Jesus? He said we will have tribulation but He will be with us in it until the end of time. He'll be in the midst of our crisis and troubles and when we call upon Him, we will see His grace at work. The more we experience troubles, the more we learn to persevere in our trials. Perseverance builds character and character cultivates authentic, sustainable hope. Simply stated, suffering is the catalyst for hope.

Suffering is a refiner's fire. That's one reason it is so effective in building character. When we undergo the fire, we find out what we're made of. The truth is, we may never know until the fire comes how we'll respond, no matter how prepared we think we are for it. Let me tell you a story in this regard.

Standing firm before the fire, a prerequisite for victorious living in a time of crisis

Living in the mountains most of my life, I have developed a great respect for the damage and devastation fire can create. I've experienced numerous forest and grass fires and have discovered a person can never be too prepared. Living on our ranch on Timber Butte, I have learned the importance of looking ahead and preparing for the potential of a devastating fire season. Preventative maintenance takes thought and work. It requires vision; looking ahead for the sake of knowing what to do if disaster happens. Preventative maintenance requires both physical and mental preparation. It requires thinking through how one will respond or react mentally and emotionally before hardship is on the doorstep. You may never know for sure what you'll do, but determining your options in advance will help. Will I run from the crisis or stand and fight?

We have lived at the base of Timber Butte for nearly ten years, and in that time Nancy and I have experienced five close calls with range fires. We have good reason to know how vulnerable we are. Living so far out in the country, it often takes a while for help to reach us. In the case of a lightning-caused fire, it can take up to an hour for professional firefighters to arrive on the scene.

Every spring, we disk a large swath around our buildings to form a thirty-foot firebreak. We keep flammables away from the structures and landscape with minimal combustible-type plants. We have a 500-gallon fire tank mounted on a trailer fitted with fire hoses and a pump. We have a backup generator in case of a power outage, which allows us to run our well, enabling us to refill the fire tank. We keep the fire trailer hooked to a ranch pickup all summer long, so no time would be lost scrambling to get things together when the inevitable happens. Nancy and I have had to become our own volunteer fire department. All of this preparation is good, but unless a person is fully committed to stand before an approaching wall of flames, all is for naught.

In 2014, a fire did sweep across our ranch. It started on our neighbor's property on a hot, windy afternoon. I had just finished working for the day and had cleaned up for dinner when I looked out our kitchen window and saw a wall of flames jump the county road into a dry pasture on our north property line. The line of fire was heading straight toward the barn and house, being pushed and energized by wind. There was no time to think, only to act.

Nancy called 911 while I quickly ran to start the truck and gasoline-powered water pump. Luckily, the horses and cows had already come into the barn from the pasture. I hurriedly shut the gate behind them and opened the gates leading to the outside fields. Nancy jumped in the farm truck and headed toward the wall of fire. I jumped on the running board of the fire-tank trailer, hanging on for dear life. By the time we got to the firebreak that protected the barn, the flames had already arrived. From that time on we did the things we had planned, more on adrenalin than with strategic skill. The flames, at first, were intensely hot, and the smoke was so thick it was hard to breathe or see, but our efforts were working. Although there was a moment I felt like dropping the hose and running, I could see we were winning. The flames started to subside just as a neighbor showed up to help. The fire parted around our buildings just as the water ran out. We took up shovels to continue the fight, watching the flames roar through our west pastures and over the distant hills. Forest Service firefighters and a volunteer fire department were a welcome sight when they arrived, but the real danger for us had passed.

Here's my point: In this life and especially in the hour we now live, fires will come. The question is not will there be tribulation in this life, but rather will we be ready for it, and even more so, will we stand firm when it comes?

Be Ready, Stay Alert, Stand Firm!

In three of the four Gospels, the Bible records the end of the age dissertation of Jesus. This is one of the best descriptions of events preceding and accompanying the end times. Before we unpack the verses, let's look at how one passage ends. It's key to the entire message.

> *"But as for that day or hour no one knows it—neither the angels in heaven, nor the Son—except the Father. -Watch out! Stay alert! For you do not know when the time will come. It is like a man going on a journey. He left his house and put his slaves in charge, assigning to each his work, and commanded the doorkeeper to stay alert. Stay alert, then, because you do not know when the owner of the house will return— whether during evening, at midnight, when the rooster crows, or at dawn— or else he might find you asleep when he returns suddenly. What I say to you I say to everyone: Stay alert!"* (Mark 13:32-37, NET).

Over and over again, Jesus exhorts His followers (as did the Apostle Paul) to stay alert and be ready for trials that come our way. Jesus also tells us the most important thing we can do when these calamities happen is to "stand firm." Matthew's account says this, *"Because of the increase of wickedness, the love of most will grow cold, but the one who stands firm to the end will be saved"* (Matthew 24:12-13, NIV.)

Nancy and I would not have stood up to the flames that threatened our ranch had we not been ready for them. To be honest, I didn't know what I'd do before that experience. I'd never faced a wall of flames that so forcefully threatened my home. From the less threatening experiences we previously had, we knew we'd have no choice but to run if we weren't prepared to face such a disaster. We did everything we knew to do physically in preparation, but it wasn't until we actually came face to face with the trial that we discovered we were up to it. Because of the trial, we now have strength and much greater hope for the challenges that lie ahead. It reminds me of the words of James, the brother of Jesus, *"Consider it pure joy, my brothers and sisters, whenever you face trials of many kinds, because you know that the testing of your faith produces perseverance. Let perseverance finish its work so that you may be mature and complete, not lacking anything"* (James 1:2-4, NIV). For those who are going to be truly victorious in the days before us, this may be one of the most important lessons. We're not talking about survival here, we're talking about victory.

What Victory?

When most of us think about the prophesied trials that precede the "end times," we think about the doom and gloom and suffering that will accompany the rising of an Anti-Christ, the tribulation, the mark of the beast, or the battle of Armageddon. Many Christians think more about survival than victory. The only victory they can see is the second coming of Jesus, but Jesus said that in the midst of the trials and suffering, the *"gospel of the kingdom will be preached in the whole world as a testimony to all nations and then the end will come"* (Matthew 24:14, NLT). It's a short sentence in the midst of a lot of painful stuff, as we'll see later, but for true, authentic Christians who have an eternal view and sincerely believe the Bible, this is huge. It's what we've been waiting for. It was the cause we signed up for when we first said "yes" to a relationship with God. What would it take for the gospel to go to every nook and cranny of the world? I can promise you one thing, it won't happen through social media. Social media is losing its credibility because almost everyone is pushing their personal agenda to the point that it has become "relative truth" or "alternative facts." Relative truth isn't truth, it's opinion. And, if you haven't noticed, these days everyone has an opinion, but they aren't necessarily true. Opinions are only " true" for the person who proclaims it. No one knows what to believe these days; everything seems a little deceptive.

How then will the Gospel get into the hearts of people all over the world? It will go with sincere, trustworthy relationships — it's the only way it can. That means a new kind of church and a new kind of Christian will arise out of the ashes of tribulation. The church will be an agency of compassion and mercy in a time when the world is crying out for help. God's love will be demonstrated through the actions of His people which will be a focus for our final chapter together.

A move of God this big will require the conditions of society to be just right. The culture will have to experience many of the things which were ignition primers in past revivals. When these conditions have reached a tipping point, there will be an eruption that will look ugly at first glance, but will, in fact, be the birthing of spiritual awakening. Possibly, it will become the final move of God before His second coming; but how could we know?

Birth pangs of the final days

- ### According to the words of Jesus

Ever since the days of the apostles, the church has been expecting the second coming of Jesus. The anticipation was based on the social climate and world events that Jesus described before His crucifixion. In those final days, He was sitting with a group of His disciples on the Mount of Olives when they asked Him what were the signs of His second coming and the end of the age. Three of the four gospels record His answer.

Jesus began His last days' dissertation with a warning; a warning He would revisit numerous times as He described events which would precede His coming. The warning was to be alert, stay on watch, and not be deceived. Evidently, one of the first characteristics of the final days was that of deception, specifically by those He referred to as anti-Christs.

He spoke of wars and rumors of wars and an increase in world violence. He said that nations and kingdoms would rise up against each other. In addition to human suffering, the physical earth would begin experiencing crisis as well. There would be an increase in natural disasters, such as earthquakes and famines, and all these things would not be the end, but rather be birth pangs leading to the end.

He spoke of an increase of wickedness, of man's inhumanity to man, and warned the love of many would grow cold. It sounds grim for sure, but in the midst of it all, He said the gospel would be preached to all nations. In the middle of all the pain and suffering, the message of His kingdom would go to every corner of the world and only then would the end come.

• According to the apostle Paul — bad human behavior

In 2 Timothy 3, Paul also provides a list of things that will one day characterize the last days. His list doesn't focus so much on world events but rather human behaviors. He warns Timothy that there will be terrible times in the last days. During those times, he says, people will become extremely self-focused; they will be lovers of themselves, lovers of money, boastful, proud, abusive, disobedient to their parents, ungrateful, and unholy. His list goes on, saying many would be without love, unforgiving, slanderous, without self-control, brutal, not lovers of good, treacherous, rash, conceited, lovers of pleasure rather than lovers of God. They will have a form of godliness but deny His power.

Wow! Sounds like a major breakdown of society — a growing culture of egocentric people looking out for number one.

- **The words of the apostle Peter — scoffers will scoff**

Peter wrote: *"Above all, you must understand that in the last days' scoffers will come, scoffing and following their own evil desires. They will say, "Where is this 'coming' he promised? Ever since our ancestors died, everything goes on as it has since the beginning of creation"* (2 Peter 3:3-4, NIV).

So then, who are the scoffers? Scoffers are people with smaller world views. They are often people who have a hard time comprehending and accepting that their world is changing. They would be ones, for example, who would deny climate change, saying the increase of weather devastation is caused by normal climate cycles, such as El Nino and La Nina, and has been going on since the creation of the world. El Nino and La Nina do impact weather on an annual basis, but they do not account for the gradual global temperature increase. One climatologist explained it with the visual imagery of an escalator. El Nino and La Nina are the stairs on an escalator that is constantly moving upward.

A huge portion of the world's population now lives in large cities or residential areas where climate is artificially controlled. Much of that population, especially in the developed world, has become desensitized to changes in nature due to the presence of forced-air heat and air-conditioned environments. They are oblivious to a gradually changing climate and are unwilling to admit there is a problem caused by human overuse of fossil fuels, because it would threaten the comfortable American lifestyle to which they have become accustomed. Many would prefer living in denial, not only concerning the issue of climate change, but to other social concerns as well. If we acknowledge issues such as extreme poverty and social injustices of every kind, then we must accept responsibility to provide solutions. If we don't, then we must deeply bury our heads in the sand of complacency.

Sadly, conservative Evangelicals are becoming identified as the leading scoffers and refuters of climate change in America today.

Climate Change: Is it a birth pang?

A warming planet will, over the course of time, cause human suffering through drought, famine, pestilence, and natural disaster. Calamities of these kinds are likely end times' birth pangs connected to a changing climate and should be seen by Christians as significant, not something to be ignored. Jesus said to keep watch, stay alert, and be aware when we see these things happening around us, not to scoff or deny them.

- **Why Evangelicals should be leaders not deniers**

Climate change is a sanctity of life issue. It puts our entire planet in peril. When glaciers and polar ice melt, oceans rise. This, combined with storm surges, flood low-lying lands, and the first to suffer are the world's poor. Throughout the developing world in places like Bangladesh, the poor are the ones forced to inhabit places others don't value. In Bangladesh, low-lying farmland is already becoming unusable due to the intrusion of rising seawater. In many parts of the world, rising seawater is forcing the relocation of many, causing a new reason for refugee migration. Even in America, a changing climate is creating havoc. The climate's warming trend is making wet places wetter and dry places drier. As oceans become warmer, climatic conditions fuel more powerful hurricanes and abnormal snowstorms. Weather is now becoming another issue threatening our national security. Over 1,000 tornadoes were reported in 2016 alone. In that year, the US experienced fifteen weather events, each exceeding one billion dollars in damages. These events included excessive drought, massive wild fires, four different flood events, eight severe storm events, and a hurricane. The 20-teens are seeing more record-breaking weather crisis years than any other century in recorded history.

This is not something to be denied by the church, but rather to be seen as an opportunity to be on the front lines. Jesus commissioned His followers to serve a broken world by bringing His message of hope; a message that can only occur by way of relational response and a demonstration of hands-on compassion.

- **"...the love of many will grow cold."**

As the earth warms and weather crises intensify, human suffering in America, and around the world is becoming a sad reality. It seems to me that every day news reports show up-close images of some new disaster caused by extreme weather events. The frequency is causing our culture to experience what is commonly referred to as "compassion fatigue." I think this may be what Jesus was talking about when He said, *"...the love of most will grow cold"* (Matthew 24:12, NLT). America is losing compassion for a world where there is a constant barrage of natural disaster and human violence, both at home and abroad. Rather than being known as scoffers or becoming a part of a culture whose love is growing cold, we must become engaged, not only in the aftermath of devastation, but in creative solutions before devastation occurs.

When there is an awakening of true Christianity in the last days, it will be led by a people willing to physically engage world crisis. This new breed of leaders and participants will take the gospel throughout the world, not just with words but with hands and feet. They will be the ones Jesus spoke of when He talked about feeding the hungry, providing fresh water for the thirsty, shelter to the homeless, and giving hospitality to the alien.

- **Living in the tension — "No man knows the time or hour... Therefore keep watch...Be alert!"**

For Christians and non-Christians alike, many feel the tension of the hour in which we live. Things are feeling increasingly less safe. After 9-11, we lost the feeling of national security we once had. In the teen years, we have experienced an increase of violence in our cities. In 2016 alone, Chicago experienced 4,367 shootings in its streets. These types of numbers are staggering and appalling, but they are nothing compared to the brutality that has transpired in a country like Syria, where woman and children have been brutally murdered and many people left without homes or possessions. In 2016, the United Nations identified 13.5 million Syrians requiring humanitarian assistance, with 6 million internationally displaced.

It is not only the violence, but the growing degradation of the global environment and the potential for a world that will not be able to sustain life as we know it. Many feel threatened by the uncertainty of our nation's political climate as we rapidly become less popular on the world's theater, even among our international neighbors and allies.

We feel the tension of an angry culture and a rapid change in ethics and values. What used to be unacceptable is now becoming the norm. Things are unraveling and it seems there is nothing anyone can do about it. It feels, in many ways, that world violence could escalate over night as more nations become equipped with nuclear armament, especially a nation as unpredictable as North Korea. Two questions are being asked: Are we nearing the end? Are these the last days? Jesus said two things: First, He said, *"But about that day or hour no one knows, not even the angels in heaven, nor the Son, but only the Father"* (Matthew 24:36, NIV). And second, He reminded us that, *"Even so, when you see all these things (speaking of the birth pangs), you know that it is near, right at the door...therefore keep watch... be alert"* (Matthew 24:33, NLT). So, if we are alert, what might we see?

This book offers two answers to the question, what can we see concerning the condition of the world as it relates to the last days? First, we can see through Chapter I an historical pattern repeating itself several times since the days of Jesus, which will end in a massive spiritual awakening. We have seen how many of the cultural conditions that birthed the Jesus Movement in the '60s and '70s exist today, but more intensely. We can also see when previous moves of God began losing energy and direction, it made room for something uniquely different and great.

Second, we looked at Jesus's description of the global conditions He called birth pangs before the second coming. It will be for the reader to decide if the conditions of our day and what we are presently experiencing are, in fact, a match of those conditions.

• Like the days of Noah...

Jesus said the last days would be like the days of Noah, in which the general culture was unconcerned and were carrying on with their lives status quo. They were doing the things they always did, eating and drinking, marrying and giving in marriage right up to the moment Noah and his family entered the ark. Personally, I'd like to be more aware. I'd like to be more observant so that all this doesn't catch me totally by surprise. Noah was aware. He prepared and was ready for what was to come. The questions are: What does that mean for us? What would it mean to be prepared? Should we stockpile food and then load our guns so we can defend our supplies from hungry neighbors? Should we find a cave and take up residence in hope of hiding from the world? Or, would it be better to pursue God with everything we have in hopes that our lives might somehow be instrumental in the greatest spiritual awakening the earth has ever known?

> ### A personal note from the author to those conservative Evangelicals reading this book
>
> Before you read on, I feel the need to pause and bring clarity to something important for my fellow Evangelical comrades. I'm about to say some things that I'm quite certain will bring strong offense and reaction to many who are reading this book. My prayer is that you will not stop reading because of personal political convictions, but will be open to think upon the motive of my message. I say this because the discussion that follows is, in fact, crucial for conservative right-wing Evangelicals to understand if they hope to impact the lives of a new generation.
>
> When it comes to Millennials, perspective is everything. In order for my generation, the Baby Boomers, to understand the mindset and worldview of Millennials, we need to realize that the vast majority of them do not see things the way we do. For this reason, many of their generation are rejecting Evangelical values and thus, Christianity all together. As a writer, I feel the need to be absolutely honest and say some things in the following pages that are even uncomfortable for me.
>
> I personally am grieved at the current political climate not only because I feel it is contrary to the heart of Christ, but because of what it is doing to the upcoming generation. I have always considered myself a conservative Evangelical Christian. I am a registered Republican and always have been. I've always voted for Republican presidents as long as I can remember. I did not, however, vote for Donald Trump in the past election but chose, as did many of my Christian contemporaries, to write-in my choice of candidate. With that said, let me continue.

Evangelicals get Trumped: The great compromise

- Johnson Amendment repeal may be a death blow

Two weeks after the president's inauguration, Donald Trump was invited to speak at the Evangelical National Prayer Breakfast. In his speech, he announced he would use his executive power to repeal the Johnson Amendment of 1954, which was cheered by those present.

While Lynden B. Johnson was a Senator from Texas, he proposed an amendment to the tax code whereby tax-exempt entities, like churches and other charitable non-profit organizations, would be unable to directly participate in political campaigns on behalf of any candidate. In other words, church leaders could not use their public pulpits to promote a political candidate running for office. The amendment was passed by a Republican Congress and signed by Dwight D. Eisenhower, a Republican President.

Exit polls indicate that 80% of eligible white Evangelicals voted for Trump and significantly contributed to his victory in 2016. It stands to reason then, that Donald Trump would be in favor of this tax code provision as he has already looked ahead to a second run for office. The repeal of the Johnson Amendment would give men like Jerry Falwell, Jr. and other conservative Evangelical leaders the right to endorse and use church resources to promote a second Trump presidency.

This may well be the final death blow to Evangelical credibility as a viable movement of true Christian faith. As we have seen throughout church history, when the church maneuvers to become a controlling political entity, the Spirit of God has a way of withdrawing. This leaves what once was a powerful work of God ineffective as an agency of faith. But the good news is God always provides a fresh outbreak of His Spirit to fill the void.

In the context of this book, my personal concern is not so much for the choices or actions made by a secular president, but rather the defining decisions made by fellow Christian leaders. My understanding of Christian history tells me I can stand with great hope and faith knowing God's Spirit is alive and well and will not leave humankind, but will certainly visit us in a fresh new way.

- ### The great Evangelical compromise

For Christians to have put their faith in the Trump candidacy required great compromise. For years, the religious right has professed uncompromising values when it came to sexual morality, faithfulness in marriage, integrity of character, and Christ-likeness in attitudes and behavior. To compromise these deep core values is to take a giant step into hypocrisy. Sadly, the unchurched world saw Evangelical Christians lay these values aside for the sake of achieving political agendas. This reinforced their already negative attitudes concerning American Christianity. Evangelicals stated they voted for the Trump campaign because the Democratic nominee was worse, forgetting they had made their choice from six other good conservative candidates, many of whom had solid track records concerning lifelong commitments to the Lord.

* * *

Sadly, the unchurched world saw Evangelical Christians lay these values aside for the sake of achieving political agendas.

* * *

- ### A litmus test for Christian leadership

For Christians, there is a litmus test for leadership. When it comes to politics, a litmus test is defined as "a question asked of a potential candidate for high office, the answer to which would determine whether the nominating official would proceed with the appointment or nomination." For the Christian, the framework for such a question can be found in Galatians 5. Here Paul provides a list of the "Fruits of the Holy Spirit." This list provides nine attributes or qualities that characterize someone who has the Spirit of God working in them. Paul says it like this:

> *"But the fruit of the Spirit is love, joy, peace, forbearance, kindness, goodness, faithfulness, gentleness and self-control. Against such things there is no law. Those who belong to Christ Jesus have crucified the flesh with its passions and desires. Since we live by the Spirit, let us keep in step with the Spirit. Let us not become conceited, provoking and envying each other"* (Galatians 5:22-26, NIV).

When a Christian is in the process of making a decision as to who they would trust to have authority over them, it would be wise to visit this list of Godly attributes. At the same time, wisdom would suggest they should reverse the list and decide which of the two best characterizes the person in question. It might look like this:

Christ-likeness	Contrary traits
Love	Self-love, egocentric, narcissistic, prideful
Joy	Instigates anger, anxiety, and depression
Peace	Instigates fear, disunity, and hostility
Patience	Impulsiveness, rashness
Kindness	Mean-spirited, bully
Goodness	Bad behavior, provoking, demoralizing
Faithfulness	Unfaithfulness, disingenuous
Gentleness	Harshness, arrogance, authoritarian
Self-control	Impulsive, without restraint

In addition to this list, Paul goes on to say, *"Since we live by the Spirit, let us keep in step with the Spirit. Let us not become conceited, provoking and envying each other."* (Galatians 5:25-26, NIV). This list reminds us what it looks like when a person is being not only led by the Spirit, but has been empowered by God for the sake of living a Christ-like life. For a Christian, a Scripture as clear as this should speak for itself and need no further commentary.

For many Americans, Donald Trump's impulsive behavior both at home and abroad are worrisome. During his candidacy, he acknowledged his immoral sexual slander towards women, his unfaithfulness in marriage, even his ability to get whatever he wants. In January 2016, he told his rally supporters he could go out on 5th Avenue, shoot someone, and not lose voters. It was a perception which reflected how he saw himself, and now, looking back, he may have been right about not losing voters, at least among Evangelicals. Again, this is not about Donald Trump, it is about the great compromise made among American Evangelicals.

- **Who's defining "Making America great *again*"?**

Evangelicals who have embraced the Trump campaign slogan, "Making America great again" should ask themselves a couple of questions: When was America great, and how is greatness being defined? America has changed. Although it was clearly founded with Christian values and principles, it is a secular nation now. Political policy and all the legislation in the world will never change that. America needs a fresh vision; a vision that looks ahead to a preferred future, not back.

It's true, America has had times of greatness. We were great when every person in our nation, men and women alike, were unified, sacrificing everything to fight and win world war victories in two different theaters at one time. That certainly was greatness!

America was great when it responded to men like Martin Luther King, Jr., putting their lives on the line for civil rights and social injustice. That was greatness. America was great when it had the reputation of being the most benevolent nation on earth, reaching out around the world with compassion and mercy. And it was great when it erected a statue called "Liberty" and posted a sign at America's front gates which stated:

"Give me your tired, your poor,
Your huddled masses yearning to breathe free,
The wretched refuse of your teeming shore.
Send these, the homeless, tempest-tossed to me,
I lift my lamp beside the golden door!"

This, too, was greatness and more than anything reflected the heart of Jesus for a nation that once declared it was, "One Nation under God."

America wasn't so great when it proclaimed "Manifest Destiny," saying God had given us the North American continent to expand and enhance its political, social, and economic influences. It gave Americans a sense of entitlement, allowing them to exploit it for personal gain. This translated into repression of the American Indian, and exploitation and abuse of wildlife and natural resources. That wasn't a shining moment for America.

There were times of greatness for sure, but much of that greatness was not necessarily translated into power, monetary wealth, or global dominance. Those things were simply by-products of a people who wanted freedom for all and were willing to work hard to maintain that freedom. God honored it.

For the Christian, greatness is translated much differently than what is on the minds of many today. For Jesus, everything was backwards and upside-down. For Him, the greatest is the least, in fact, the greatest is the servant of all. Jesus told us to love our neighbors (in this context that would be Mexico and Canada), and to even love our enemies, to do good to those who hate us. I know this may sound idealistic to some, but for a true follower of Christ who says he/she accepts the words of Jesus as life, we can't ignore this upside-down concept for living. If American Evangelical Christians truly want this nation to be godly, we might do well to rethink what a credo like "making America great again" would and should look like.

> * * *
>
> **If American Evangelical Christians truly want this nation to be godly, we might do well to rethink what a credo like "making America great again" would and should look like.**
>
> * * *

In February of 2017 while watching a news broadcast, I noticed a poster being carried by a young girl marching among a crowd of angry protesters at an international airport. They were protesting against the President's executive order to stop aliens entering the U.S. from Middle Eastern Muslim countries. I noticed her possibly because she looked different; her face looked angelic. She stood out to me because her expression wasn't like those around her who projected fear and anger. Her poster simply read: Hebrews 13:1-2. I couldn't recall the Hebrews text offhand, but because of her unique countenance, I was motivated to look it up. This is what I read: "*Keep on loving one another as brothers and sisters. Do not forget to show hospitality to strangers, for by so doing some people have shown hospitality to angels without knowing it*" (NIV). Reading this simple Scripture, I had a sense the Lord was speaking to me - this wasn't only His heart, but is the heart of a new generation. Out of the ashes of fearful protest would rise a movement of beauty and of authentic, God-inspired greatness.

Revisiting Maslow's hierarchy of needs in the 20-teens

Maslow's hierarchy of needs
1. **Basic** — air, water, food
2. **Safety** — feeling secure
3. **Love** — Intimacy, family, friends
4. **Self-esteem** — significance, respect, being wanted and needed
5. **Self-actualization** — fulfillment, personal development, fulfilling life's purpose

Life at the top of Maslow's pyramid may well be like living on the roof of a house of cards. For the most part, life in the United States has been good, especially for those of us who have enjoyed growing up in the middle and upper-classes of American culture. We've never missed a meal, we've had a roof over our heads, and since the mandatory Vietnam draft of the 1960s ended, we haven't been forced to go to war. As world history goes, it doesn't get much better. Revisiting Maslow's hierarchy of needs, the majority of Americans have been living in the upper tiers of the Pyramid. Most of the suffering we have experienced has been on those upper levels, striving to be loved and accepted, wanting to be valued and needed, and desiring to understand our place in the world. Our needs have been more emotional and psychological than physical. Crisis and suffering for us has been more of suffering from human rejection, feeling unloved, and unvalued than from life-threatening issues such as starvation, thirst, or genocide. Living on the upper tiers of the pyramid often makes people introspective and self-focused, which is generally a formula for unhappiness.

Nancy's and my life of ministry work has provided us with opportunities to experience many poverty-stricken regions of the world. It has taken us to the jungles and cities of Asia, Africa, South and Central America, and to remote islands in the South Pacific. We have seen some of the most severe poverty and human suffering on the planet, and in our travels, there has been one thing which has astounded us: how happy people, especially children, in the developing world can be. These are people living on the bottom two tiers of Maslow's pyramid. In these places, there are few therapists or psychologists dealing with people's inner-child issues. Not that those issues aren't real and genuine needs, but because they haven't been given the luxury to think about them. All of their energy and thoughts are given to obtaining clean water to drink and food to feed their families. I think these, the most vulnerable, may well be the ones Jesus was speaking of when he said, *"...Blessed are you who are poor, for yours is the kingdom of God. Blessed are you who hunger now, for you will be satisfied, blessed are you who weep now, for you will laugh"* (Luke 6:20-21, NIV). People living on the upper tiers of Maslow's pyramid often lose sight of their need for God, while those at the bottom need Him every day just to survive. It may be those who live with greater crisis will in the end be the most blessed. If that is the case, America may be entering a season whereby people will recognize their need for God's intervention.

Many are becoming aware of some very real problems arising on the not so distant horizon. Because of living on the upper tiers of the pyramid, many have failed to notice or care about the erosion taking place on the foundational tiers. If the foundation continues to weaken and crumble, the whole pyramid could collapse. What I mean is there is a lack of awareness concerning growing environmental problems affecting American agriculture and our clean water supply. Let me start with agriculture.

Is global hunger on the horizon?

America has been a major agricultural provider, not only for our own nation and nations willing to pay for our diversity of exports, but has also been a leading provider for international relief efforts. Our ability to maintain food security is not merely a national concern, but a global one. America has been blessed with an abundance of rich soil and fresh water, and the preservation of these precious resources is a matter of survival for a world approaching 8 billion people. At first glance, our present condition looks amazingly good. America has increased the quantity of its food production at a steady rate over the past thirty years. Much of this increase is a result of genetic engineering, the use of powerful new chemical herbicides, pesticides, and artificial fertilization. The problem with American food production is not a matter of quantity, but quality; not only quality, but a growing fear by many of non-sustainability. There are many reasons for this concern, but I'll highlight four:

1. Corporate agriculture and the GMO takeover

GMO stands for genetically modified organism. In the world of agriculture, it is a plant that has been genetically altered through biotechnology. GMO seed production is relatively new in America, having only become widely accepted and adopted by American farmers since the turn of the last millennium. This transition from conventional farming practices happened very quickly. In the US, by 2010, over 90% of major crops, such as soybeans, corn, and cotton had become GMOs. In 2013, approximately 54% of crops were genetically modified throughout the developing world.

The purpose of GMO engineering is to introduce new traits into plants which do not naturally occur in the species. For example, genetic engineering can now create plants resistant to certain pests and diseases. It will also enable plants to be resistant to drought, reduce spoilage, and provide a resistance to targeted chemical treatments. This would include a resistance to toxic herbicides, such as glyphosate, otherwise known as Monsanto's Roundup.

Some would say that we could not feed today's world of 7.5 billion people without the use of GMO technology. They would also claim that the day of organic food production, at least on large scale, is over. Others would emphatically deny this claim, saying GMO technology is the beginning of the end for sustainable global food production.

2. Quality vs. quantity and the impact on human health

Because GMO technology is relatively new, it has taken awhile to determine the long-term effects on human and animal health. Nearly all wheat, corn, and soy beans grown in America are now GMO. Since the relatively recent GMO takeover, there has been a noted increase of gluten intolerance as well as surges in autoimmune diseases in populations consuming these products. Many Americans are no longer even feeding their pets GMO foods due to the noticeable adverse effects on the animals' skin and hair.

Let's consider that most major crops are now considered "Roundup Ready". That is to say, they are sprayed multiple times with the toxin glyphosate as a means of eliminating unwanted weeds. Roundup is so lethal it kills anything growing except the GMO crop itself. Many would say this can't be healthy no matter how many tests agricultural scientists conduct. More and more consumers, aware of the health issues connected with modern agricultural practices, are now insisting on organic foods exclusively. The problem with organic foods, whether they be cultivated plants or butchered livestock, is that they are relatively expensive. And, unless people produce their own foods (plants and animals) or purchase it from a reputable local farm, they cannot be assured that it is truly organic. It is becoming increasingly more difficult for city dwellers to avoid GMO food and impossible for the poor to afford organic.

3. The GMO monopoly — the danger of one corporation controlling the entire global food market

GMO food is grown with hybrid GMO seed. Hybrid seed was initially developed after WWII along with artificial, chemically produced fertilizers. Hybrid seed is produced by crossbreeding two varieties of plants for a preferred new strain. There are two potential big problems with hybrid seed. One, hybrid seed will not reproduce itself. In other words, if you grow tomatoes using hybrid seed, you cannot use the seeds from the resulting new tomatoes to grow more tomatoes. Hybrids are dead ends. They are like a mule. A mule is the result of crossbreeding a horse and donkey; mules are sterile and cannot produce offspring of their own. A hybrid plant is the same. So why is that so dangerous?

Farmers who grow hybrid or GMO crops are forced to go back to the seed producer every year to buy new seed. Until WWII, farmers produced their own seed from their previous year's crop. Farmers had practiced their own seed production since the beginning of farming, but after WWII, modern agriculture had become dependent on the corporation which supplied their annual seed needs. In today's world, that corporation is Monsanto, and some would say Monsanto has an agenda to become a global monopoly on seed, and thus have control of global food production. If you ask me, that's scary.

The second issue with hybrid seed is that it has lost diversity. Many activists are busy saving and storing original seed varieties of all types of plants. They are even locking them away in special frozen storage vaults in the event of global catastrophe. Modern agriculture is robbing the earth of its once rich food diversity. This, too, is sad and a concern because these foods have survived every kind of climatic change and have stood the test of time.

4. Rapid soil loss due to overuse and chemical poisoning

Another concern for the future of global food supplies is soil loss. When western pioneers came into the Midwest in the 1800s, they discovered what appeared to be an endless prairie of rich grasses. This great "sea of grass" was supported by three feet of dark, enriched soil, soil that had been fertilized by countless buffalo herds migrating across the prairies and rich sediments left after centuries of flooding. This, too, was a national treasure. For the next one hundred years, settlers developed small family farms and became the breadbasket of America. They fertilized their farm land year after year with manure from the family chickens, hogs, and cattle, spread across their fields by means of horse-drawn or tractor-pulled mechanical manure spreaders. The crops they produced were 100% organic, and the soil remained rich.

At the end of WWII, a great discovery was made. America had huge surplus stockpiles of chemical nitrogen which had been used to produce the bombs that defeated our enemies. The need to figure out a way to eliminate these toxic piles inspired the idea of using it for agricultural fertilization. It worked. In fact, it worked so well that farmers who refused to use it could not compete with the production of those who did, especially with corn. As a result, the Midwest was changed forever. There was so much corn produced new uses for it had to be developed. For the first time, it became feed for animals that previously had only eaten grass, and eventually, it became a means for ethanol fuel production. As corn agribusiness expanded, large corporations bought out the small family farms and began using new farming techniques. Massive machinery plowed and harvested the land, while chemicals became the new norm for fighting insects, killing weeds, and fertilizing crops. The soil that was once so rich in nutrients and organic material was becoming poisoned and stressed. As the climate began changing, unprecedented rains fell, causing flood waters to top river banks. Over time, top soil and toxic chemicals washed into rivers and were carried to oceans. The rivers and oceans suffered from chemical pollution, and the soil began to decrease in depth and richness. All this happened in less than a hundred and fifty years, leaving us with the questions: How long can such a non-sustainable process last? How long can American farmland feed the world if there aren't drastic changes? When Jesus said that famine will be a birth pang, is that day drawing near?

- ## Water, water everywhere, but hardly a clean drop to drink!

The World Water Council's vision report recently stated, "There is a water crisis today. But the crisis isn't about having too little water to satisfy our needs, it is a crisis of managing water so badly that billions of people — and the environment — suffer badly." In today's world, water is a growing point of international tension. Some have predicted that in the future, more wars will be fought over fresh water supplies than over remaining non-renewable oil and fossil fuel reserves. Even in our present day, one out of six people do not have access to safe drinking water. That's 1.1 billion thirsty people!

97% of the earth's water is in the form of salt water in the oceans. This leaves only 3% remaining as fresh water. Three-fourths of that remaining 3% is locked up in glacial ice, trapped in deep, underground aquifers, or in the form of vapor found in clouds. The remaining 1% is stored in lakes, man-made reservoirs, rivers, and reachable aquifers. Sadly, much of that final 1% is polluted beyond drinkable use.

Of this available, reachable, fresh water, fully 66% is extracted from rivers and aquifers for agricultural use. In arid regions, that number is 90%. 34% is used for domestic household use while 10% is used for industry. 4% is lost from reservoirs through evaporation.

Two hundred sixty river basins are being shared by two or more nations in the world today, and although underground, many countries are forced to extract water from a shared aquifer. Many of these nations are not friendly to each other, and for them to remain cooperative concerning agreeable water-rites and usage is becoming increasingly more difficult.

With so many people on the planet who share so many needs, the management of fresh water is another growing challenge the human race is now being forced to face. Like the needs for food and air, water is on the foundation block of Maslow's pyramid. Though few Americans think about it and take its availability for granted, it may well be one of the first things to cause a devastating fracture in the foundation stone of America's well-being. Who would have guessed, even twenty years ago, people would be willing to pay almost as much for a plastic 12-ounce bottle of drinkable water than a gallon of gasoline? It proves that water is already considered a more valuable commodity than fossil fuel.

Consider the value of water. As a nation, we should unite and do everything in our power to protect it from environmental degradation. Consider how hydraulic fracturing (or fracking) jeopardizes subterranean aquifers. Most people understand fracking as a relatively new method of underground well-stimulation used to extract oil and natural gas. The process requires high-pressure injection of fracking fluids. These fluids consist of 90% water and aluminum oxide, plus a 10% mixture of approximately twelve chemicals, some of which are considered highly toxic. The fluids are injected into the well bore in order to fracture and break up deep rock formations, allowing natural gas and petroleum to be released. Fracking was developed as a means of extracting otherwise unreachable deposits of fossil fuel, and it has become one of the leading environmental controversies in the nation. Hundreds of law suits have been filed and won due to health problems in households whose well water has been compromised. Besides the pollution of ground water, a growing body of evidence indicates fracking is responsible for the increase of earthquake activity as well. The questions we have to ask as a nation is at what point will we value fresh, drinkable water above an increase in fossil fuel production? How valuable is water?

Much more could and probably should be said about the threat of this very precious resource. We could speak of the Standing Rock Indians in South Dakota who spent the winter of 2016 and 2017 living in subzero temperatures in canvas tents and tepees in protest against an oil company's pipeline which threatened their source of drinking water. Or we could talk about the water crisis in Flynn, Michigan, where over 100,000 people were exposed to levels of lead so dangerous they were told they couldn't even use their tap water for washing their hands. These are two highly publicized events, but they are merely the tip of a growing iceberg. We live in a world where many have not yet come to grips with the importance of environmental stewardship in a world headed for non-sustainability.

When we consider the loss of clean water and its specific impact on the world's poor, we can better understand the words Jesus spoke when He said, **"***I was thirsty and you gave me something to drink,* "adding, "*Whatever you did for one of the least of these brothers and sisters, you did for me*"** (Matthew 24:35-40, NIV). Jesus knew over two thousand years ago where the earth and humanity were heading.

Cultural disjuncture — tremors of "Awakening"

The 20-teens are filled with new and growing concerns. It's no wonder that our nation is experiencing growing outbreaks of fear and anger. As one Senator put it, "There has not been so much energy in the streets of America since the Vietnam war. "Our culture is on the brink of becoming unraveled. Citizens are crying for justice, honesty, and solutions; they blame government officials for playing shell games and creating polarization and disunity. Citizens are overwhelmed, angry, and scared, looking for answers and relief from deep, underlying stress. They are not unlike the people who felt suppressed and overlooked during the days of Luther and Wesley or, in a lesser way, during the 1960s.

The world is on the threshold of a great eruption, and the tremors of that eruption are being felt most deeply in the grassroots of the culture. America will begin to experience growing movements of resistance and cries for revolutionary change, but these movements will not be ones driven from the top. They will rise from the grassroots of the culture, being led by a new generation who will hopefully look to God for their marching orders.

- **Leaders who build bridges not walls**

If there is to be spiritual awakening, it will neither be Protestant nor Catholic but a type of Christianity that is free of restraining barriers or boundaries. A spiritual awakening of such magnitude will require leaders with hearts so full of love and compassion, their vision would look far beyond the present walls of exclusiveness with bridges that span the turbulent waters of fear and hatred. They would see all men as equals in God's eyes, taking the biblical words, "*God so loved the* (whole) *world that He gave His only begotten Son....*" (John 3:16, NASB). This new breed of leader will emerge from the Millennial generation, but will have received their cues from leaders who have gone before them; leaders who boldly communicated these values even while they were unpopular. Pope Francis is an example of a leader who has proven to be courageous, compassionate, and aware of the world he lives in. He is a bridge builder and a beacon of light.

Only a captain who sailed along the coasts of rocky shores before the time of modern-day navigational systems could fully appreciate what a beacon of light on a dark, stormy night could mean. It was not only a light, warning of danger, communicating where not to go, but was a light that provided assurance and direction. A beacon light is not always appreciated or even noticed during the light of day, but becomes a means of life in times of dense fog, turbulent waters, and moonless darkness. As culture gravitates towards a season of darkness, shining lights will illuminate to provide comfort and hope.

* * *

Pope Francis is an example of a leader who has proven to be courageous, compassionate, and aware of the world he lives in. He is a bridge builder and a beacon of light.

* * *

Even in the Evangelical world I live in, I have noticed a quiet trend toward Catholic values. Not the formality and religiosity of Catholicism, but the root motivations of some of its early founders. Saint Francis of Assisi, the father of the Franciscan Order, and Ignatius Loyola, father of the Jesuits are two such heroes of the Catholic faith. Both had extreme passion for an intimate and authentic relationship with Jesus. Both fought courageously against the system for the sake of illuminating a pure and simple devotion to God. Both had compassion for the poor and an awareness of the world in which they lived. Both shared creative minds that welcomed ingenuity for the sake of reaching the world with God's unconditional love. Saint Francis had a deep love for the natural world, recognizing it as God's workmanship. Concerning nature, he once said, *"These creatures minister to our needs every day: without them we could not live; and through them the human race greatly offends the Creator. We fail every day to appreciate so great a blessing by not praising as we should the Creator and dispenser of all these gifts."* St. Francis was an environmentalist.

Both St. Francis and St. Ignatius Loyola, were known as men of solitude and devotional meditation. Both men saw the value of musical creativity and how important it was to the human spirit. For Protestants and Catholics alike, men like these today serve as role models for those desiring a life of deeper spirituality combined with an outward ministry to a broken world. In the past few years, I have observed many Christians (mostly from a younger generation than my own) gravitate towards the Ignatius style of prayer which emphasizes imagination, contemplation, and personal application.

It might be in part because of St. Frances and St. Ignatius Loyola that the latest Pope has gained so much favor and respect in the world. The Pope adopted his new name "Francis" when he accepted the responsibility as Pope. He took this name from his life hero, St. Frances of Assisi. Pope Francis is of the Jesuit (Ignatius) Order. He has both intentionally stated and proven through his actions to be a Christian leader who reflects the compassionate characteristics of the Franciscan and Jesuit Orders.

Pope Francis practices what he preaches concerning his heart's desire to not be enamored with position and prestige as some Popes have in the past. His heart is to be a bridge builder between God and man (the word "Pontiff" or Pope actually means "bridge builder"). After the Pope's visit to the US and Mexico in 2016, he was asked by the media what his thoughts were concerning the proposed wall between the US and Mexico. He responded by saying, "*In the social and civil context as well, I appeal not to create walls but to build bridges. To not respond to evil with evil. To defeat evil with good, the offense with forgiveness. A Christian would never say 'you will pay for that.' Never. That is not a Christian gesture. An offense you overcome with forgiveness. To live in peace with everyone.*"

Pope Francis's address to the United States and the United Nations in September 2016 exhorted everyone to take immediate action against the devastation that climate change is bringing upon the earth, and especially to the world's poor. He emphatically stated that the causes of climate change are produced by man's sinful nature and are an injustice to the world's disadvantaged. He stated, "*The misuse and destruction of the environment are also accompanied by a relentless process of exclusion. In effect, a selfish and boundless thirst for power and material prosperity leads both to the misuse of available natural resources and to the exclusion of the weak and disadvantaged, either because they are differently abled (handicapped), or because they lack adequate information and technical expertise, or are incapable of decisive political action.*" This is a key point as we close this chapter and move toward the final chapter concerning the rising spiritual awakening. Pope Francis's heart and courageous exhortations will be a key ingredient for reaching the unchurched world with the love and provision of Christ. He is a role model, not recognized by many non-Catholic Christians, but will be one of many prophetic voices speaking into the hearts and minds of the emerging "new lights" — a rising generation of Christ-following revolutionaries.

Part III

WHAT WILL BE

The Awakening

The 1920s had distinctiveness; so much so that it was characterized with a name, the "Roaring 20s." It is marked as a transitional moment in American history: a moment where the "great American dream" became redefined. WWI came to an end, and the country mourned its losses but celebrated its new role on the world theater. We had become a global might and a leader in innovation; the automobile became modernized, the airplane commercialized, household appliances mechanized, musicians and movie stars idolized, and the culture liberalized. It was a season that expressed itself with fresh cultural norms; classical music turned to "Big Bands," traditional dance turned to the Charleston, and prohibition was disregarded as religious fanaticism. America had changed forever. Now, nearly a hundred years later, the year 2020 has the potential of becoming yet an era of notable transition and distinctiveness. It will either be the beginning of America's unraveling or the catalyst for a major spiritual awakening. The verdict is still out.

In 2020s the Baby Boomer generation, which has composed forty percent of the US population, will all be washing up on to the beaches of retirement like a great wave, many without the prepared resources to do so. The majority will be relying almost solely on remaining social security reserves for survival, adding stress on the United States' economy. At the same moment, there will be a massive transitional handoff from Baby Boomers to Millennials, not only of a great national debt load, but of major leadership roles for industry, the corporate world, government, and the church. A torch will be passed; a torch that once may have burned bright, but will likely only be a flicker. The Millennials will inherit the results of the Boomers' heyday of living out the "great American Dream" as was redefined a hundred years before.

In 2020, the Millennials will be in their twenties and thirties. They will be the new, dominant, adult generation. Like the Boomers of the 1960s, many have totally rejected the faith of their parents. 2 out of 10 Americans under age 30 believe attending a church has no worth. Fifty-nine percent of Millennials who were raised in church by their Boomer parents, have dropped out during the "20-teens." Thirty-five percent have an anti-church attitude. They will be inheriting a nation in financial, environmental, and social crisis without a relationship with God to fall back on, unless, in utter desperation, they rediscover authentic faith. I believe they will. I believe something very beautiful will come from these ashes. I believe what the enemy means for evil, God will turn to magnificence. I believe the "new lights" will shine.

Moses is dead! — a changing of the guard

When I was 57 years old, I felt the Lord spoke a word to me. He said it was a time for my generation to experience "youth-anasia." I didn't believe this meant euthanasia as in physical death, but in order for the church to become youthful as it had been during the Jesus movement, my generation of leadership would have to die to self. We would have to give up control and pass the baton to the generation below us. Some were calling this generation "Generation X," but whatever they might be called, they are the present-day leaders and trainers of the Millennials.

At two o clock one morning I woke up out of a dead sleep. Knowing that trying to fall back to sleep was fruitless, I walked down stairs and sat in a chair where I habitually spend many hours of solitude. It wasn't long before I heard Nancy's steps coming down the stairs. She joined me saying she, too, couldn't sleep. I shared with her my word and together we decided it was time to begin a seven- year handoff transition as lead pastors of our church. We had founded the church nearly twenty years before and had loved the process and the people. At 57, I still felt young and vital. I still had vision for the work and couldn't imagine what I'd do or how I might reinvent myself. In my mind, I wasn't ready to retire or end a life of ministry, but I also knew it wasn't all about me. Little did I know, as I approached my 65th birthday, the last year of the lead-pastor transition, I would be diagnosed with prostate cancer. In the same year, Nancy and I became the primary care givers for both my parents who were suffering from Alzheimer's and extreme dementia. Both passed away the following year. Clearly, God knew things I couldn't have known. With so much on my plate, there would be no way I could lead a large church effectively.

They say pastors often attract people like themselves. Baby Boomers can relate with Baby Boomers. They share similar life experiences and world views. They liked the stories I told, and got my sense of humor. Gen Xers liked me, but they saw me more like a father or grandfather rather than a peer, and because of that, year by year the church got more and more gray hair. It needed to be "youthanized."

The next day I invited my youth pastor, Trevor Estes, to have coffee with me. He had no idea what was coming. I totally caught him by surprise, telling him of my seven-year plan to handoff the church to him. For most people, seven years sounds like a long time, but I wanted to do it strategically and responsibly. The Vineyard of Boise was a large, active church with a huge infrastructure of facilities, staff, and volunteer workforce. To drop it in the lap of someone who had only observed the level of leadership and management skill it took to run a large, complex organization, would have been sudden death for him and the church.

I gave Trevor one year to make a commitment. I told him I wouldn't tell anyone during that time so he could have total freedom to back out. The Vineyard has an Episcopal form of government (meaning the senior /visionary leader had the freedom to choose his own successor much as an entrepreneurial founder of a business would).

After the year had passed, Trevor and his wife, Andrea, accepted the challenge and we took the transition to the next phase. I shared the plan first with our elders, then with our paid staff, then with the remainder of church leaders, and finally with the church itself. This process took another year to complete. Trevor took a seat next to mine at staff and elder meetings. Over the course of the next two years, I continued to lead as normal as he watched. He often led in my place when I traveled or was absent. I think it was about the fourth or fifth year when he began to take the lead while I sat in the second seat (always chiming in my opinions and giving my input). Little by little, the staff began to fully accept his new role, even though I was present. In this way, we weaned the church leadership, and eventually the church itself, from my senior pastoral role. In the end, the church stayed healthy and carried on its mission to our community and the world. It hardly missed a beat, though we lost a number of Baby Boomers who gravitated toward other churches led by Baby Boomer pastors. At the same time, the church began attracting young families and regained the youthfulness that birthed it in the beginning.

Trevor wasn't a Millennial, but was closer to their generation and could better speak their language. He got their humor and understood their needs. He addressed controversial social issues that Millennials deeply care about, such as homosexuality, in sensitive, biblical, and loving ways.

As the end of the transition approached, Trevor and I shared the pulpit, alternating weeks. We team taught through a common series. One of those series was the book of Joshua. The Book of Joshua was Trevor's idea, as it had become special to him personally. It was the story of transition from one generation to the next. In the first verse of the first chapter, it is announced that Moses was dead. Moses is dead and Joshua is commissioned by God to lead with strength and courage.

That's how the transition begins. The last chapter of Deuteronomy tells us that Moses's eyes, "…**were not weak** nor **his strength gone**" (Deuteronomy 34:7, NIV), but he died and was buried in an unmarked grave on the side of Mt. Moab. He came to a place where he could look out across the Jordan River and see the land that God had promised him years before. Moses had done his job, he had finished his work. Moses was dead, but his vision would be carried on by a courageous leader of a new generation, the Joshua generation. Moses was dead, and it was clear — I was Moses.

Now, there are two ways I could take this. I could have become introspective and gone in search of some really anointed inner healing, or I could feel a deep sense of privilege for having had the opportunity to run my leg of the race. The good news was, I wasn't really dead. For sure, a part of me had to die; I had to die to my own feeling of personal importance. I also had to die to self, die to being in control, die to the esteem I had always enjoyed as being our congregational leader. I had to die to the honor of being the one who would seek God for the church's direction and vision. I had to die to a lot of stuff, but at the same time I knew God wasn't done with me and I felt good about the fact that Nancy's and my withdrawal had clearly been an act of obedience. By my doing it voluntarily, I   not only kept the church moving ahead, but allowed us to stay a part of the congregational family. It put me in a position to take on a grandfather role. By not being pushed out, as many aging pastors are, I could feel the freedom to just relax and become a part of the family.

Not all transitions like this one end on such a happy note. Here are some reasons why: First, most Baby Boomer pastors don't realize how old they really are. At least they don't realize it until it's too late. Successful transitions take time and thought, and more than once I've watched as pastors wake up one day, usually after a church conflict of some kind, and realize they are tired. They realize too late that they aren't having fun anymore. In a state of distress, they pull the retirement trigger too late, leaving the church in panic mode. A second reason is that many, if not most, aging pastors realize too late that they don't have the financial resources to retire. When they were young, they had the misconception that they would stay in their pulpits until Jesus returned, and therefore neglected to build a retirement fund. They hold on to their roles for monetary reasons rather than calling or passion. Church folks are often loyal and resist change anyway, causing the church to lose momentum and youthfulness. The entire

* * *

It put me in a position to take on a grandfather role. By not being pushed out, as many aging pastors are, I could feel the freedom to just relax and become a part of the family.

* * *

church ends up with gray hair. Better to pass the baton when you're still running your leg of the race at top speed. Anyway, even if we Baby Boomers acknowledge it or not — Moses is dead!

Moses is dead, and God is about to do something exciting — He is about to raise up a new generation to not only take the flickering torches we pass, but, if we are obedient to let go, He will blow on them with the powerful wind of His Spirit, igniting a great fire of spiritual awakening. The Millennials are the hope.

Crossing over: Characteristics of the Joshua generation

• Not a singular journey, but one taken in community

Teaching through the book of Joshua, the first thing I realized was how different this new generation was from my own. Baby Boomers loved visionary, dominant leaders who pointed the way with assurance and authority. We loved strong leaders who looked like they had all the answers, even if they didn't. Our journeys were singular in nature. As a leader, I spent hours in solitude, seeking God's direction for the people He had called me to lead. It was my responsibility and I took it seriously. Baby Boomers like that. They respected it, and, depending on their level of trust in me, they followed. It was the right thing for the season in which we led, but the Millennials aren't buying it.

They seem to be less impressed with catchy credo visionary statements and five- year plans than the Boomers are. What they want is action. They want input and, if moved enough, they want to participate. They prefer doing ministry in the context of community more than independently. Relationship is a high value. If they are to cross the Jordan, they will do it together.

- **Discovering Truth**

If the Millennials find truth, it most likely won't be through preaching but by way of discovering it for themselves. When the Joshua generation watched the raging waters of the Jordan part, and then, within days, saw the walls of Jericho supernaturally crumble into a heap before their eyes, they discovered how real God was. It was only then that they fully believed God had given them a land of milk and honey. They discovered truth, and that truth changed everything.

If there is to be a spiritual awakening which will change American culture, and if Millennials are to lead it, then a new church form will certainly emerge. That new church form will have a different look, as it always did in revivals of the past. The question is: how will it look? We can only guess, but one thing for sure; it will undoubtedly reflect the Millennials' quest for authentic community and take a form conducive to a discovery process of knowing what is true, pure, and right.

Let me suggest a picture of the attributes of a Christian community of truth. I will use the acronym TRUTHS.

A Christian community of TRUTHS
T — Trust
R — Relevant
U — Unconditional
T — Tenacity
H — Hope
S — Supernatural

- **Trust**

For the Millennial, a Christian community of truth will be one of **trust**; one that is believable, reliable, faithful, and authentic. For them, this is often in opposition to what they observe in the society they were raised in. Winning trust for them will be difficult after living in a world where there seems to be no absolutes, stability, or assurances. Marriages fail, vows are only made to be broken, and the word politics has become synonymous with disunity and dishonesty. In a world where broken promises are the norm, an authentic community of trust will be magnetic.

It would be a place without hype, not one where people are tempted to manufacture God's presence through human effort. There would not be the "routinization of charisma," but only what is authentic and real. It would be a community where people could confess their questioning of God, or their struggles with personal faith, without fear of condemnation. It would be a community where the truth of God's character, attributes, and will would be openly reminded and encouraged. A place where one is challenged to believe His truth, regardless of personal or cultural circumstances.

- **Relevance**

A community of trust would also demand **relevance** by caring about things of importance. It would have to discuss controversial issues without political correctness or bias. It must be one full of grace for brokenness, a place of care and concern. It must be open to the discussion of real life issues: how to hold on to relationships, what to look for in marriage, human sexuality, money, body image, all in the context of knowing who God is and understanding His heart. It also must be relevant concerning living in a world where there is injustice, extreme poverty, and human suffering. Most importantly, it must be a place to be heard.

- **Unconditional**

Being engaged in a Christian community of trust would have to be one of **unconditional** love; a place where people could come with all their quirks and addictions, not fearing rejection or judgment. It would be a place where people would listen and not give criticism or casual advice without earned permission. It would be a place to cry without embarrassment, and a place to stumble, fail, and try again. A place where Jesus is real and present, and His healing is always at hand. A community of trust is a community where diversity is valued; where gifts and talents are accepted and encouraged. It would be a community without prejudice, where there are no dividing walls of race, color, or ethnicity.

- **Tenacity**

A community of trust is a community of **tenacity**. A place that doesn't go away, but will stand firm through times of struggle. A community that is stable, steadfast, and driven by authentic passion. Tenacious passion will be the glue that gives a community of truth a reason to stand. It is a place where passion for serving God is not just a fleeting idea, but something worth sticking to, something worthy of giving one's life for. Millennials have had the reputation of going from one thing to the next, lacking stick-to-itiveness, of not being a tenacious generation. The reason for this is they often lack a sense of true purpose and the passion to fight for something important. All this will change as they choose to become the Joshua generation, crossing over the present-day Jordan as a unified community of truth and purpose.

* * *

> Millennials have had the reputation of going from one thing to the next, lacking stick-to-itiveness, of not being a tenacious generation. The reason for this is they often lack a sense of true purpose and the passion to fight for something important.

* * *

- **Hope**

The book of Hebrews tells us "...*faith is the assurance of things hoped for, the conviction of things not seen*" (Hebrews 11:1, ESV). Faith requires tangible qualities, things like assurance and conviction (which is also translated evidence), qualities which can be observed, witnessed, and touched. But, faith also requires intangible qualities — hope and the unseen. Faith is the ingredient that makes an invisible God visible, and hope is the bridge which brings us to a confident assurance of His reality. Hope changes everything. It gives us the fortitude and resolve to make a difference in the world. A community of **hope** is a fellowship that imparts life and empowers us to live it with direction and purpose. If a community of Christian believers one day rises up to be used as a catalyst for spiritual reform, they will be an agency of hope.

- **Supernatural**

And finally, and most importantly, a Christian community of trust is a community that pursues and embraces the presence of God and His **supernatural** intervention and direction. It is a community that puts its full trust in God. Its existence is marked by those who are in a relentless quest to know, love, and serve God.

A lesson learned on a journey from Shittim: Mercy, justice, and humility

While teaching through the book of Joshua with Trevor (we alternated Sundays), I unexpectedly discovered something. I'd taught through the Book of Joshua at least twice in my thirty-year career as a Bible teacher but bumped into something I had never seen before. Chapter three opened with the sentence, *"Early in the morning Joshua and all the Israelites set out from Shittim and went to the Jordan, where they camped before crossing over"* (NIV). When I read the word "Shittim," it caught my eye. As a kid I really struggled with dyslexia, and even to this day the accurate pronunciation of Hebrew words can throw me. I always hate humiliating myself, especially from the pulpit. When I prepare messages and come upon a word like Shittim, I give it extra examination. A word like that could get a guy like me in trouble!

Wanting to know more about Shittim, I went to my Exhaustive Concordance and looked it up. There, I found it referenced in only one other place in the Bible. In Micah 6:5 it read, *"Remember your journey from Shittim to Gilgal, that you may know the righteous acts of the LORD"* (NIV). Now that was interesting because the prophet Micah was speaking seven hundred years later about the events that transpired in Joshua 3. The Joshua generation was about to leave Shittim, cross the Jordan river, and camp in Gilgal. It was a short journey, but a significant one. Micah was rebuking the Israelites right before they entered into seventy years of Babylonian captivity. He was questioning the Jewish people, asking them to recall a lesson they had learned many years before in their history. In his questioning, Micah went on to ask in verses six and seven what they learned. He asked the questions, *"Should we bring him burnt offerings? Should we bow before God Most High with offerings of yearling calves? Should we offer him thousands of rams and ten thousand rivers of olive oil? Should we sacrifice our firstborn children to pay for our sins?"* (NLT). The inference here is an unequivocal NO! Micah said that these were not things God desires. These were not things which show a man's faithfulness. The questions then are, what does the Lord want of His people, and what would show faithfulness? Micah gave the answer in verse eight, *"...the LORD has told you what is good, and this is what he requires of you: to do what is right, to love mercy, and to walk humbly with your God"* (Micah 6:8, NLT).

God's heart for this generation was, and is today, to do the work of justice, show mercy and compassion, while walking with humility. These things will bring a clear distinctiveness to the *birthing* of a new spiritual awakening. It will be a move of compassion, mercy, and justice , not of anger or rebellion, but one characterized with the humility of Christ.

Compassion, Mercy & Justice:
A distinctive for a fresh move of God

In Matthew 24, where Jesus gave His dissertation on the end of the age, He concludes with three parables in a row. One is found in the last verses of chapter 24 and the other two in chapter 25. All three provide pictures of what will happen when He (Jesus) suddenly returns unannounced. The first deals with a steward whom he leaves the responsibility of his family and estate while taking a journey. In this parable, the master comes home unannounced and judges the servant based on how well he cared for his people and land. This was a parable about doing what is just.

The second parable tells the story of ten bridesmaids who were taking lamps to meet the bridegroom. Five were foolish and five were wise. Five stayed alert and prepared while the other five did not. They didn't even have enough oil to keep their lamps burning. When the bridegroom (Jesus) arrived unannounced, only the five who were ready — those waiting in anticipation — were taken with the bridegroom.

The third was the parable of the talents. This story told of a master (Jesus) leaving his three servants with bags of money (representing talents or abilities). It says that he gave to the first five bags, to the second two bags and to the third, one bag. It says he gave them their amounts according to their abilities. When the master returned, he rewarded them according to how well they invested what they were given. This is the story of how well we, as God's people, use the things we are given by God: our talents, gifts and opportunities. Some will squander these things because of a misconception of who God is and what He desires. On the other hand, some will be good stewards, using the life they have been given well. In the final verses of chapter 25, Jesus defines what a well-invested life looks like.

Chapter 25 concludes with a picture of judgment day. Here Jesus paints a picture of people being separated as a shepherd separates sheep and goats, placing sheep on his right side and goats on his left. To those on his right he will say, *"...Come, you who are blessed by my Father, inherit the Kingdom prepared for you from the creation of the world"* (Matthew 25:34, NLT). Giving explanation to the criteria by which this separation would be decided is found in the verses that directly follow: *"For I was hungry, and you fed me. I was thirsty, and you gave me a drink. I was a stranger, and you invited me into your home. I was naked, and you gave me clothing. I was sick, and you cared for me. I was in prison, and you visited me"* (Matthew 25:35-36, NLT).

The text goes on to tell how the righteous would then ask, *"Lord, when did we ever see you hungry and feed you? Or thirsty and give you something to drink? Or a stranger and showed you hospitality? Or naked and give you clothing? When did we ever see you sick or in prison and visit you?"* (Matthew 25:37-39, NLT). Jesus would reply, *"...I tell you the truth, when you did it to one of the least of these my brothers and sisters, you were doing it to me!"* (Matthew 25:40, NLT). Two points here: One, ministering acts of compassion, mercy, and justice are a form of ministering unto Jesus himself. They are in a sense, a form of worship. Secondly, they may be a prerequisite for spending eternity with Jesus.

Many of us are so familiar with these verses that we may miss their impact. These declarations may be some of the most crucial and sobering verses concerning man's ultimate destiny found in the Gospels. Some Evangelicals will surely struggle with this thought because it indicates that doing good works could be a game changer when it comes to salvation. But, remember what Paul said, *"For it is by grace you have been saved, through faith—and this is not from yourselves, it is the gift of God— not by works, so that no one can boast. For we are God's handiwork, created in Christ Jesus to do good works, which God prepared in advance for us to do"* (Ephesians 2:8-10, NIV).

There is no question we have been saved by grace through our faith. That seems clear, but because we are God's handiwork, we were created in Christ to do good works. Not only that, but these works were prepared in advance for us to do — we are actually predestined to do them. So how does that translate into the real Christian life? It means, if we are truly followers of Christ, our spirit is programed to engage in ministries of compassion, justice, and mercy as outlined by Jesus in Matthew 25.

In order to fully grasp this, we have to recognize that the passages in Matthew 24 and 25 are all connected and all about living as if in the last days. They are all about being authentic followers of Jesus right to the end. First, Jesus describes the events and circumstances surrounding the last days. Then, He tells us to be alert and aware. As Peter put it, don't be scoffers or deniers. Next, Jesus gave three parables reminding us to be good stewards of His people, His earth (His estate), and the special gifts and opportunities He gave us as people. Finally, He tells us that to do works of compassion, mercy, and justice to the least (the world's poor and oppressed) is as if we're doing them unto Him. These acts are important when it comes to eternal destiny.

If there is to be another great awakening, those who will lead and participate in it will surely partner with Jesus in this struggling world. When Jesus quotes Isaiah 61 at the very beginning of His public ministry, He told those who were present that He was the fulfillment of this messianic missional statement.

"The Spirit of the Lord is on me, because he has anointed me to proclaim good news to the poor. He has sent me to proclaim freedom for the prisoners and recovery of sight for the blind, to set the oppressed free, to proclaim the year of the Lord's favor" (Luke 4:18, NIV).

If this was the ministry of Jesus, and if He commissioned us to carry on His work until His second coming, then this is our job description as well. Compassion, justice, and mercy will no longer be things the Christian church will push back on, but will become a major distinctive among a people who desire to engage in a coming move of God.

- **Environmental stewardship is a ministry of justice, compassion, and mercy**

Forgive me for overstating the obvious, but before closing this thought, it is crucial not to miss this point. When Jesus said that by us providing water to the thirsty, food for the hungry, and giving care for the sick was a ministry unto Him, it is crucial for us to understand these things all require an earth that has clean water and the ability to sustainably grow healthy food. 80 % of infant mortality in the developing world is related to unhealthy food and undrinkable water. These things are not merely environmental concerns, they are ones which demonstrate our passion for the sanctity of life itself!

- **Smaller footprint / Bigger handprint**

In 2008, I wrote a book based on a teaching series I had done the year before. It's not often, but every now and then, I like a series well enough to think about turning its message into a book; this was one of those times. The title of the seven- part series was, "The Biblical Quest for a More Simplified Life." One of the seven messages I preached during the series I called "Small Footprint, Big Handprint." The message stood out to me because I realized, and wanted to convey, the idea that downsizing one's life for the sake of simplicity by itself is an empty endeavor. It's good to make a smaller footprint, especially an environmental one, but it is equally important to make an impact (big handprint) with your life.

I say this because as I look at the direction the world is going, there seems to be little balance. Many have little concern about their footprint, especially their carbon footprint; they just keep living status quo lives, not thinking about how they could use their gifts for the sake of making a lasting difference (big handprint). Not to sound too negative, but I do believe the world looks at the church and believes we hold this perspective. In many cases, it is not an accurate perspective. I know how much good Christians do in the world, but I believe for revival to happen, how we are perceived by the world must change.

* * *

It's good to make a smaller footprint, especially an environmental one, but it is equally important to make an impact (big handprint) with your life.

* * *

Nonprofits, such as World Vision, Food for the Hungry, and Habitat for Humanity lead the world in providing benevolent aide of every kind. Churches all across the country have food pantries and recovery programs. There are hundreds of nonprofits all around the world doing wonderful work among the poor in the name of Christ, both Protestant and Catholic. Lots of Christian people are making big handprints for sure, but much of it is being done through nonprofits rather than through local church efforts (We discussed the reasons for this in Chapter I - *"The rise of the para-church — filling the gap"*).

Here is the point: one third of the world's population professes that Jesus is God. That is to say, 2.5 billion people in the world are Protestant or Catholic and would consider themselves Christians. If that many people actually believed and demonstrated a small footprint and a big handprint, what a difference it would make! As I already noted, Pope Francis has this value and has been using his leadership position and authority to bring it to present-day Catholicism. Not only does he have a heart for the world's extreme poor (big handprint), but he sees the need for the Catholic Church to help lead the way in reducing carbon emissions (small footprint). Evangelical churches, on the other hand, have a poor track record concerning their stand on both environmental and social justice concerns and are, in many ways, responsible for the world's perspective of Christian irrelevancy. As a new expression of Christianity emerges for the sake of becoming instrumental in spiritual awakening, lost biblical values must be regained. This new culture will no longer be perceived as scoffers of environmental degradation, or as a people who have little regard for issues of social justice, but rather as champions for promoting both small footprints and big handprints. Once again, as it was in past revivals, the church will regain its voice as an agency of relevancy as it reclaims neglected biblical values.

Grasping the Millennial worldview

- **Hope's story**

Nancy and I decided to give our second car, a ten-year-old Subaru Forester, to our granddaughter, Hope, when she turned sixteen. About four months before her birthday, our daughter Kate's car broke down and, being a single mother, found herself in a bind. Not only did she need transportation getting to and from work, she had to get Hope around as well. The simple solution seemed obvious: we could lend the car to the girls, putting it in Kate's care, and later grant Hope the title on her sixteenth birthday. All went well until Kate got her vehicle fixed and Hope became the primary operator of Nancy's and my car. It was summer at the time, and Hope was a volunteer worker for a ministry I had started at church called I-61.

I-61 is an abbreviation for Isaiah 61 (which speaks of the messianic commission of Jesus to the broken world), and is a ministry focusing on training people to engage in world crisis issues. We have a training / mission base established in Nicaragua, but our main office is in Boise. Hope worked with the I-61 staff two days a week and used our car to get there. Everything was going great until one morning I noticed a strange bumper sticker on the back of what I still considered my car. When I saw it, my blood pressure escalated to dangerous levels. Maybe you've seen it.

With the word "Coexist", the sticker displays seven different symbols representing seven different spiritual ideologies; Islam, Wicca, secular science, Judaism, Buddhism, Yin-yang, and last, but hopefully not least, Christianity. From my Evangelical worldview, the sticker gave a very clear message — there are many ways to God. To say the least, I was really ticked off and it didn't take me long to let Hope know how I felt.

I called Hope into my office, sat her down, and first reminded her on whose car she had attached that bumper sticker. Second, I told her what the bumper sticker meant, in case she didn't know, and third, told her to take it off. She was hurt, and told me I had misinterpreted the meaning of the sticker. To her, it was a message of world peace saying that everyone should get along. In fact, to her it was clearly a Christian message that reflected the heart and attitude of Jesus.

As an Evangelical pastor, the idea that Jesus is the only way to God has been and will always be my primary message. That won't change, but what did change was a better understanding of the Millennials' mindset. Hope did take the sticker off because she understood my view and how important it was to me, but, over time, I learned to listen to her more and value her perspective. What I realized was, she had not only been raised her whole life in church, but in the church I pastored. I've never questioned her faith in God, or her sincerity to follow and even serve Him. The lesson I learned was how she, like so many of her generation, after being raised in church, could translate biblical truth so differently than most Evangelical Baby Boomers. The questions are: how did that happen, and, is it important?

- **If Jesus lived today, would the Millennials view Him as a liberal?**

Just that question alone is enough to set most Evangelicals into a frenzy. If you feel the hair rising on the back of your neck, this next section is probably for you, but there's no point in going further if you're not willing to put the glasses of a Millennial on first. Also, you need to understand that truth to a Millennial, especially when it comes to politics, is arrived at through a combination of observation, feelings, and perception. The conclusions they ultimately reach might be accurate or not, but to them it is truth.

Like my granddaughter Hope, many Millennials have grown up in Christian environments hearing about the heart and character of Jesus. Many attributes which characterize the ministry of Jesus and biblical truth are in direct conflict with what they are hearing and seeing in today's conservative political camp. Let's look at a few examples:

- **Concerning the poor**

There should be no question in any Christian's heart concerning what Jesus felt, and what the Bible teaches, about the poor. Luke 4 tells us Jesus came to proclaim good news to the poor. The topic of the extreme poor and the commission to serve them is a front and center mandate of Christian truth. It is also perceived to be a primary value of the Democratic Party. Thousands of Millennials swarmed to hear Bernie Sanders speak as a presidential candidate because of his passion to help the "least of these" in America. He was the hero and the candidate of choice for most Millennials who had become fully engaged in the 2016 election. Right or wrong, in their minds, liberals cared more for the poor than conservatives, especially when it came to issues like immigration, injustice, and the environment's impact on suffering humanity.

- **Concerning issues of human rights and injustice**

According to Jesus's pronouncement in Luke chapter four where He said He had come, *"…to proclaim liberty to the captives and… to set at liberty those who are oppressed"* (ESV), it appears Jesus cares deeply about issues of injustice against the oppressed. God is a God of justice. This truth is found from one end of the Bible to the other. If you doubt this, go read Isaiah 58. This section of Scripture expresses God's heart for the poor and oppressed. It also tells how much God opposes religion that goes through all kinds of motions but neglects the care for the poor and downtrodden. Social justice is biblical justice. Some have wrongly confused social justice with socialism. Socialism is a form of government, and is, in itself, oppressive and self-serving. It does not reflect the heart of Jesus.

* * *

The topic of the extreme poor and the commission to serve them is a front and center mandate of Christian truth. It is also perceived to be a primary value of the Democratic Party.

* * *

Here, too, Millennials perceive Democrats as being more compassionate, having greater mercy, and being more civil minded. In Christian terms, they might even say liberals are more Christ-like. In a present-day event, the Standing Rock Indian situation in South Dakota might serve as an example. Many would point to this situation, where a minority group of people are protesting against a powerful oil company in an attempt to protect their native lands and water from inevitable pollution.

Here, too, Millennials could perceive the Republican Party as being an uncaring oppressor.

Even as I write this, four African countries are enduring a devastating drought, putting millions of people in a state of extreme risk. The epicenter of the crisis is in Somalia, where half of the country's population is suffering from starvation and water contamination. One hundred and ten children are dying each day from dysentery and other waterborne diseases. This devastation and loss of life is happening at a time when America is pulling back financial and humanitarian aid in the name of "Making America great again" and "America first." Reflecting on Matthew 24 and 25, we recall Jesus saying that in the last days there would be extreme famine in the world. We will also remember, at the same time He commissioned the righteous to feed the hungry and provide water to the thirsty, saying that as we do it to the least of these (Somalia being the least), we are doing it unto Him.

* * *

This devastation and loss of life is happening at a time when America is pulling back financial and humanitarian aid in the name of "Making America great again" and "America first."

* * *

For those American citizens who perceive themselves as being "the righteous" Jesus spoke of, these words should sting right now. Millennials may well take up the plight of the extreme poor, especially if they perceive their government becoming an agency which is turning its back on global human injustice and   suffering.

- **Concerning creation's care**

Conservative Christians have a growing reputation for having little concern for creation's care. By many, they are perceived as anti-environment. When Paul writes to the Romans in the first chapter, he says, *"For the wrath of God is revealed from heaven against all ungodliness and unrighteousness of men, who by their unrighteousness suppress the truth. For what can be known about God is plain to them, because God has shown it to them. For his invisible attributes, namely, his eternal power and divine nature, have been clearly perceived, ever since the creation of the world, in the things that have been made. So they are without excuse"* (Romans

1:18-20, ESV). What Paul is saying here is that all the attributes of God can be seen through His creation, through nature and the earth's environment. The environment is a picture of the nature or attributes of God, and when man sees it in its natural state, he/she has no excuse for not knowing who He is. We call it nature, because it reveals the nature of God. When it becomes defaced, people will get a distorted image of God. If anyone should have the reputation of keeping nature pure, it should be those who say they care about presenting God to a lost world. The creation is the best form of introducing people to the nature of God. Nothing shows His "invisible attributes, His eternal power, and His divine nature" better. So again, we have to ask ourselves, who has the better reputation of caring for or being the greater advocates for creation's care, conservatives or liberals?

Very few Millennials would deny the reality of climate change. They see it both as caring for the environment, and an issue of survival on the planet. 2016 had been the hottest year on record, and was the third year in a row to set heat records, largely due to rising C02 volumes caused by man-made emissions. The newly appointed Environmental Protection Agency (EPA) director by the Trump administration, Scott Pruett, has denied the evidence provided by 2,000 intergovernmental panelists who submitted proof that climate change was a result of human activity. As Millennials observed America's EPA losing thirty-eight of its programs due to major budget cut backs, and the rejection of commitments to the Global Paris Climate Change agreement, they became disheartened with right-wing politics. As oceans rise and storm surges continue to devastate lives, who do you think they will look to for hope? I'd say it will be those who have fought the hardest for environmental regulations and reformation.

- **Concerning hospitality to the alien**

When Jesus taught about the separation of the sheep and the goats in Matthew 25, He talked about issues which were closest to His heart. If you recall, when He said, "*I was hungry and you fed me, thirsty and you gave me something to drink,*" He also included, "*I was a stranger and you welcomed me*" (ESV). Then, when being asked by the righteous, "*When did we see you a stranger and invite you in?*" He responded, "...when you did it to one of the least of these my brothers and sisters, you were doing it to me!" (ESV). As was mentioned in Chapter II, the United States has the reputation of inviting and providing hospitality to the foreign alien. This characteristic of our democracy, along with being champions of the poor and the oppressed, has given us the justification to call ourselves a Christian nation. The reason thousands of American citizens are marching against harsh immigration restrictions is for this very reason. Because we are becoming motivated more by fear than love, we are rapidly losing our global image as a nation of benevolent hospitality. Here again, as Christian Millennials observe changes in our government, which they see to be discriminatory to race and religion, they place the blame on conservatives. Banners in protests have read, "What would Jesus say?" It's a good question.

- **Concerning free will, the First Amendment, & freedom of the press**

Another issue of cultural change our nation is presently experiencing, by way of the executive branch of our government, concerns an aggressive push-back on the freedom of the press. For the president to openly say the press is the enemy of the American people is not only wrong, but scary! The First Amendment, which our founding fathers wrote into our constitution, was based on the biblical Christian principle of free will. This amendment not only assured our citizens the freedom of religion, speech, and the press, but also granted the right for peaceable assembly (to speak out grievances against our government). The amendment stated these things would be essential for us to retain freedom.

* * *

For the president to openly say the press is the enemy of the American people is not only wrong, but scary.

* * *

The God of the Bible is a God of free will. He is a God that, in His wisdom, knew that in order for man to receive His love and choose to follow Him, we would need the freedom of choice. We need the right to say yes or no. It's the only way love can really work. America was founded on this basic truth, and that is what makes America unique and great. The reason communism is evil is because its goal is to rob people of free will.

For a Millennial to understand this basic truth and to perceive it as a threat to freedom, who do they blame? Millennials are entering their most vibrant adult years. They are coming into a time when decision making is on the forefront of their lives, and at the same time, having to sort out many mixed messages concerning faith. Many perceive right-wing conservative Evangelicalism as the definition of the Christian faith. It is tragic to realize how that perception, right or wrong, will cause so many to throw the baby (Christ) out with the bathwater (right-wing politics).

Equipping the Re:Form-ers

- **Key to Christian development and world impact**

Historically, every major move of God had a method of developing grounded, mature disciples. Without a system of discipleship, there would be no way to keep up with the rapid growth and expansion of the work. A movement needs leaders who share the values that birthed it and sound biblical training, so even as the revival expands rapidly, they will be able to recognize any potential for heresy. As we recall from Chapter I, Methodists received their name because John Wesley provided a "method" of discipleship, equipping young men to carry his expanding work to the world. St. Ignatius of Loyola, the priest who began the Jesuit Order, did the same thing as he realized how rapidly God was expanding the global work of the Jesuits. If there is to be an awakening in the season before us, the same intensity of discipleship and leadership equipping must be in place. This move of God will be unique in nature, and will require a method or process that will fit its culture. Although no one can claim to know exactly how it will look, we can observe historical patterns and cycles, and overlay lessons from the past on present-day culture and world conditions. We can also lean on our life experience and ask God to give us prophetic insight. The point of this book is to provide a framework to do both.

- **Re:Form — a new form**

Training programs, to be effective, must be understandable, thorough,

119

and reproducible. They must take nothing for granted, taking every willing participant from beginning to end concerning the Christian faith and life. It is the only way a body of Christian believers could be united in values and work together to achieve the kind of result that would carry the gospel to every nook and cranny on the globe. It sounds overwhelming, but it has been done in the past, and will surely happen in a much greater way in the future. Spiritual awakening demands spiritual reformation. To "re-form" means to achieve a new form; a new form yes, but one with truth fully intact. This is the job of equipping the Saints for the work of a fresh new season of ministry.

- **The birthing of a new season for a new harvest**

Spiritual awakenings occur when the old form becomes broken, distorted, dysfunctional, or ineffective. Jesus said it like this, *"...unless a grain of wheat falls into the earth and dies, it remains alone; but if it dies, it bears much fruit"* (John 12:24, ESV). In movements of God, it appears that the old order of things must pass away for new things to arise. Old seasons fade into memory as new seasons come, bringing new life. Spiritual hunger occurs when harvest fields ripen as the growing season finally reaches fruition. If the cycles of church history hold true, and if the culture has been cultivated and prepared through uncertainty, confusion, and struggle, and, if a generation is hungering and the Lord is willing, then America is ready for its harvest fields to *rise*.

Romans 12: Consecration, Transformation, Participation, Reformation

No matter what kind of equipping takes place in a spiritual awakening, it must reflect a complete process of Christian development beginning with being spiritually birthed in Christ, and ending as a full participant in spiritual reformation. There is no place I know of in Scripture which outlines this process better than Paul's exhortations found in Romans chapter 12. Here, Paul walks us through four phases of Christian development: consecration, transformation, participation, and reformation. As we briefly walk through this process, I will demonstrate why this will be so powerful in the context of a spiritual awakening led by the Millennial generation.

- **Consecration — Phase 1:**

> *Therefore, I urge you, brothers and sisters, by the mercies of God, to present your bodies [**consecrate yourself** - dedicating all of yourselves, set apart] as a living sacrifice, holy and well-pleasing to God, which is your rational (logical, intelligent) act of worship* (Romans 12:1, AMP).

A decision for Christ may start with every eye closed and every head bowed and the uncertainty of a raised hand, but discipleship begins with the full-on consecration of a human life. It must be a clear decision to dedicate one's self to be set apart as a living sacrifice to God, to His purposes, and His service. It's not a one-time event. Paul told us to, "...*continue to work out your salvation with fear and trembling, for it is God who works in you to will and to act in order to fulfill his good purpose*" (Phil. 2:12-13, NIV). It's a big deal — a life commitment to a lifelong process. Consecrating one's life to this process is a rational act of worship, one that ignites a spiritual transformation of thinking, behavior, and life direction.

* * *

Coming from a culture that has only known relative truth, noncommittal vows, and bouncing from one ideology to the next, an act of consecration is completely foreign.

* * *

This is true of anyone, but for a Millennial, it's huge. Coming from a culture that has only known relative truth, noncommittal vows, and bouncing from one ideology to the next, an act of consecration is completely foreign. With it, they will not only be granted purpose and direction, but something worth far more — something to live for. It's the first step of the journey and to understate it or in any way minimize its meaning is to encumber the other three phases. It is something to be recognized and celebrated.

- ### Transformation — Phase 2:

And do not be conformed to this world [any longer with its superficial values and customs], but **be transformed and progressively changed** *[as you mature spiritually] by the renewing of your mind [focusing on godly values and ethical attitudes], so that you may prove [for yourselves] what the will of God is, that which is good and acceptable and perfect [in His plan and purpose for you]* (Romans 12:2, AMP).

The second phase of the journey toward Christian maturity and functionality is transformation. It is a time of changing worldviews, giving the believer an upside- down and backwards paradigm of life. Coming to Christ fully is disorientating and can be confusing. It is a supernatural event that could never occur through human effort. Superficial values and actions begin to have no meaning. Desires and attitudes change; what once was O.K. is no longer O.K. Attitudes driven by conformity to a secular culture won't work anymore. God begins giving the new believer glimpses of His heart and mind, igniting new and deep emotions, often combined with unexpected tears. They begin to understand how God sees them, how He has always loved them, which is usually in direct contradiction of how they see themselves. The Spirit is at work not just transforming the mind, but the heart as well. The walls the world has forced them to build as a means of protection from rejection and pain begin to crumble, leaving them vulnerable and feeling weak. But, because God uses weakness to build strength, a new boldness and sense of passion begins to emerge. Because of this, many react without maturity, causing new convictions and passions to become misdirected by not having yet discovered God's will. This is a crucial time for close mentoring and accountability to the community.

It is during the transformation phase that one of the most important events in the Christian experience should occur, but sadly, is too often passed over. For any believer, but especially for the Millennial, this is a paramount moment in the journey. It is the time in which we, as followers of Christ, are meant to discover why God created us. To discover, *"[for yourselves] what the will of God is, that which is good and acceptable and perfect [in His plan and purpose for you]"* (Romans 12:2, AMP).

Life is a miracle. It is a privilege we have been granted, the gift of having the opportunity to walk the earth for a short time. Life is not an accident. There are no accidents with God. No matter how you were conceived, no matter what the circumstances, you are not an accident. Not one person born into the human race would have been given this amazing gift if it hadn't been ordained. You were put here on this earth for a purpose. And, not only were you put here, but you were put here at this moment in human history. You have been given a destiny and the one thing that will give your life true meaning is the discovery and pursuit of that destiny. The questions of the ages are: What is my purpose, why am I here, what should I do with my life?

Other than introducing people to a life in Christ, one of the most important functions of the Christian community is to help people fully experience the transformation process and discover God's good, pleasing, and perfect will. This includes issues of self-image, personal value, a sense of belonging, accurate self-perception, God-given gifting, and harmonious functionality in the Body of Christ.

* **Participation — Phase 3**

> *"For by the grace [of God] given to me I say to every one of you not to think more highly of himself [and of his importance and ability] than he ought to think; but to think so as to have sound judgment, as God has apportioned to each a degree of faith [and a purpose designed for service]. For just as in one [physical] body we have many parts, and these parts do not all have the same function or special use, so we, who are many, are [nevertheless just] one body in Christ, and individually [we are] parts one of another [mutually dependent on each other]. Since we have gifts that differ according to the grace given to us, each of us is to use them accordingly: if [someone has the gift of] prophecy, [let him speak a new message from God to His people] in proportion to the faith possessed; if service, in the act of serving; or he who teaches, in the act of teaching; or he who encourages, in the act of encouragement; he who gives, with generosity; he who leads, with diligence; he who shows mercy [in caring for others], with cheerfulness"* (Romans 12:3-8, AMP).

Functional participation in the Body demands sanctification. Paul starts this third phase, the phase of participation, by exhorting us to "not think more highly of ourselves than we ought, but to have sound judgment." This means to walk in humility and to pursue Christ-likeness. This is an act of sanctification. It is a work that only God can do in us, but one in which we must be willing and open to whatever it takes to get us there. Most often it doesn't come easy. It requires total surrender, and in more cases than not, the work of God's refining fire. This part of the process also requires the support of a community where there is unconditional love, honesty, and trust.

As the quality of sanctification begins to emerge (we are all a work in process), it is time to match purpose, gifting, and destiny with functionality in the body. Without this, the body becomes uncoordinated and immobile. The church is only as effective as the gifting and harmonious participation of its people. This is the responsibility of the people and of those that are called to lead. Paul encourages us to become dependent on one another, while yet doing the things we were created to do in harmony with all the other parts according to the grace given to do them. Easier said than done. When Paul says, *"...we have gifts that differ according to the 'grace' given to us, each of us to use them accordingly,"* this indicates that for this to happen it will require a divine work of God (grace) and some human intention to *"use them accordingly."*

There are two great enemies which constantly are at work trying to dismember the Body of Christ: independence and codependence. This is true of both the members and the leadership. When people operate in independence, the body becomes disjointed and non-functional. When leaders are codependent or overcontrolling, the body loses freedom to move altogether. This, too, is an issue of sanctification.

Paul gives some examples but not a conclusive list of body functions. Some seem more supernatural in nature than others, but all are God given. None are more important or crucial for functionality than others; they are all needed and all require a level of faith. The short list includes prophecy, service, teaching, generosity, leadership, mercy, and cheerfulness. I believe Paul's intention is to not make an all-inclusive list, but to show how important diversity is in the makeup of the church, and how everyone, no matter what their gifting, is both needed and important.

Consider the thought that cheerfulness is a gift equally as important as prophecy, leadership, or any of the others. God has created every human uniquely; no two are alike. Power comes when people don't become isolated or pigeonholed, having the will and opportunity to bring their uniqueness and differences to one table. This may well be a reason the Millennials will do well; they are a generation that value and will embrace God's vast human diversity.

- **Reformation — Phase 4**

"Love is to be sincere and active [the real thing—without guile and hypocrisy]. Hate what is evil [detest all ungodliness, do not tolerate wickedness]; hold on tightly to what is good. Be devoted to one another with [authentic] brotherly affection [as members of one family], give preference to one another in honor; never lagging behind in diligence; aglow in the Spirit, enthusiastically serving the Lord; constantly rejoicing in hope [because of our confidence in Christ], steadfast and patient in distress, devoted to prayer [continually seeking wisdom, guidance, and strength], contributing to the needs of God's people, pursuing [the practice of] hospitality.

Bless those who persecute you [who cause you harm or hardship]; bless and do not curse [them]. Rejoice with those who rejoice [sharing others' joy], and weep with those who weep [sharing others' grief]. Live in harmony with one another; do not be haughty [conceited, self-important, exclusive], but associate with humble people [those with a realistic self-view]. Do not overestimate yourself. Never repay anyone evil for evil. Take thought for what is right and gracious and proper in the sight of everyone. If possible, as far as it depends on you, live at peace with everyone. Beloved, never avenge yourselves, but leave the way open for God's wrath [and His judicial righteousness]; for it is written [in Scripture], "Vengeance is Mine, I will repay," says the Lord. But if your enemy is hungry, feed him; if he is thirsty, give him a drink; for by doing this you will heap burning coals on his head." Do not be overcome and conquered by evil, but overcome evil with good." (Romans 12:9-21, AMP).

The end product of the Christian journey, at least the part we live out on earth, is to be an agent of reformation; an agent of cultural change. As was previously stated, reformation is to re-form. To re-form is to bring forth a new form, a new expression, a new paradigm. In the final verses of Romans 12, Paul describes the heart and transformed mindset of a true Christian reformer.

In the first half of this section, Paul exhorts us to practice mature Christian attributes. These are issues of the heart. The heart of a reformer is one devoted to sincere, authentic love, one that loves justice and abhors evil, and is passionate, zealous, and full of spiritual fervor for the service of the Lord. He describes a person who radiates joyful hope, one who is not a stranger to persecution and suffering because he has learned to be patient in it. A reformer is a person of prayer and of Christian hospitality, sharing with people in need, not being afraid to associate with people in less fortunate positions in life. They are people full of true ministry, "*Rejoicing with those who rejoice and mourning with those who mourn*" (AMP). As Paul concludes this list of mature Christian attributes, he finishes with living in harmony and humility and not being proud or conceited. At the end of the journey, the believer arrives at a place of selflessness and other-centeredness. Ultimately, this is landing perfectly in the middle of God's good, perfect, and pleasing will.

* * *

When our minds became spiritually transformed, we began to see the upside-down kingdom Jesus continually taught. This is a kingdom diametrically opposed to the kingdom of the world.

* * *

In the final verses, Paul reminds us to translate our transformed thinking into practice. When our minds became spiritually transformed, we began to see the upside-down kingdom Jesus continually taught. This is a kingdom diametrically opposed to the kingdom of the world. This is a kingdom where the first is the last and the greatest is the least and the greatest of all is the servant of all. It is here that Paul reminds us not to repay evil for evil, to bless those who persecute us, to not curse them, to not take revenge but leave it up to God to justify us, to feed and give water even to our hungry and thirsty enemies, and in general, we are to overcome evil by doing what is good. These are not just behavioral attributes of a reformer, but outward responses and actions. Paul has described the kinds of people that will indeed change an angry, out-of-control world. These people are the hope of a great spiritual awakening.

- **Reformers challenge the status quo**

Reformers are individual people who will courageously challenge the status quo and take action against it. It was once said of Martin Luther, as he challenged the powerful and corrupt Catholic system of his day, "He was one ordinary person who stood up to authority for what he believed no matter the cost." Many reformers had been tortured and burned at the stake as heretics before him, but because he was so passionately committed to his cause, he was willing to put everything on the line for it. Reformers see hypocrisy and social contradiction and can't remain passive. They see wrong thinking and wrong doing and become outraged, while others accept acts of injustice as simply the way things are. Luther, for example, recognized the simplicity and humility of Jesus and the apostle's lives, while observing the extravagance of the church, and the luxurious lifestyles the bishops and priest enjoyed at the expense of the poor people who supported them. He saw it as an injustice and was outraged to the point of action.

Not in the box ... not out of the box — a whole new box!

At the birth of the Jesus Movement revival, there was so much pushback on traditional church nobody wanted to meet in a venue that resembled it. The first churches met in homes, but when participants grew in number, new places were sought out. Facilities like gymnasiums and converted warehouses were favored gathering places. The church Nancy and I first attended met in a large, concrete fairgrounds facility. We constructed a plywood stage for the worship band and dozens of homemade bistro-type tables filled the auditorium. The place had concrete block walls and a concrete floor. It was ugly and cold, but it was unique and totally non-traditional. We thought it was cool. Most of the church members were either single or newly married with no kids. Nancy and I were older than many (still in our 20s) and had two small children, and even though the

RE:FORM

building wasn't kid friendly, we brought them to nearly every gathering with us. They sat with us at a small round table and colored or just hung out on the floor. We had a large portable room on wheels at the back of the hall that had a large front window. It was for parents with crying babies and we called it the "penalty box." Looking back at it now, by today's standards it seems kind of sad, but during the time it was happening, we accepted it as a normal community experience. Somehow our kids survived and eventually made lots of friends; singles got married and added to the kid population, all of which eventually led to creating a children's ministry.

- **Changing the dress code and venue**

Another form of pushback motivated by traditional church was a strong emphasis on not having a dress code. It's hard to realize after so many years have passed, how everyone once dressed so formally for church. The Jesus Movement undermined so many traditions! Our credo was, "Come as you are — you'll be loved," and people did. I remember every spring our pastor would teach a message on proper dress for the hot summer months, in order to help the young men not stumble. We never took a formal offering because it, too, reminded us of the traditional churches we grew up in. We placed Kentucky Fried Chicken buckets at the exit door for people to leave tithes and offerings. I remember bringing my parents to our church for the first time and watching them go through culture shock. I felt for them in a way, but for us, it had already become a new normal, and for our kids, and eventually their kids, it became downright traditional.

A few questions: If there is to be a new form of faith that is in reaction to a perceived traditional expression of present-day religion, what will it look like? How different will it be? There's no way of really knowing, but based on what I know of Millennials, I have a few thoughts.

- **Beer, wine, coffee, and Jesus**

My first guess is that Millennials will be motivated to gather in places conducive to embracing the unchurched. Most Millennials won't so much gravitate to what they perceive as church-like facilities. That was true in the Jesus Movement days too, but we ended up just creating a different type of church facility. As unconventional as they seemed to us, they were still church facilities. Millennials may gravitate toward something altogether different.

Remembering that Millennials don't respond as much to a lecture format of teaching but retain more through self-discovery, the new form of church they may adopt will be more relational, meeting on a regular basis in much smaller groups. As we say in our church, "we gather in rows and in circles." What that means is we meet in rows on Sunday in a lecture setting, but midweek in circles. When we say 'in circles' we mean around a table or in someone's living room in small, facilitated, discussion groups. I believe Millennials will gravitate more to circles than rows even though they will likely gather in rows as well. If they build facilities or campuses, the layouts of these meeting places will reflect functionality and relationship. Benevolence centers, vegetable gardens, recreational areas, and playgrounds will be conducive for young families working together while serving their communities. Kitchens and eating areas will be a must as the church will reflect a large family unit.

Our desire as Baby Boomer pastors and leaders had always been to get our people outside the church walls into the community, but the Millennials may decide not to have any walls to begin with. Boise, Idaho is a capital city with a very fun and creative culture. It's not a big city, but a city all the same. It has a population of about 300,000 people. In the city, as small as it is, there are 20 to 30 brew pubs and a dozen wine shops, as well as who knows how many Starbucks- type coffee houses. These may be the new meeting venues for the church. Brew pubs and wine tasting shops are not bars. They could never be compared to the bars we knew growing up as Baby Boomers. Bars were often dark, sinister places, conducive to drunkenness. Pubs are light and friendly. It is rare to find any level of drunkenness in a brew pub. Brew pubs are places where Millennials consider specialty beer an art form. Brew pubs are not places where boys shop for girls but places of friendship; places to sit around tables, discussing issues of life. They are places where Millennials gather, both Christians and non-Christians alike, seeking common ground. They are places where people can have genuine fun yet be honest and real.

Martin Luther once said, "Ale houses make the best churches." He also was quoted when talking about spiritual warfare and his personal struggles with Satan, "Whenever the devil harasses, seek out the company of friends, joke, drink more, and make merry." Luther was the father of the greatest reformation since Jesus and it sounds like he would be the first to endorse the idea of holding church in brew pubs.

When non-Christian people come into a church setting, the peer pressure is clearly for faith in Christ. To share any view other than a Christian one is often so intimidating, most are afraid to be honest with feelings and opinions if they differ from Christian ideology. As a result, many come and hide, sometimes for years, never feeling the comfort to admit who they are, what they believe, or where they've been. A pub is a place of common ground. In a pub, the Christian is often in the minority, motivating them to express their beliefs in non-religious ways without religious language. I may be wrong, but if Millennials are to lead the way in a fresh move of God, whatever they do will not be done within the confines of the traditional box. It will not be done in the box or even out of the box, but rather, without even realizing it, they will build a whole new box.

Characteristics of the Re:Form movement

- **Prophetic voices**

Reflecting back on previous discussions concerning religion and politics, Millennials are also seeing contradiction, illogical thinking, compromise, and inconsistency between what Evangelicals say they value and the way they vote. In many ways, Millennials have seen biblical values being championed more by Democrats, who have been demonized by many conservative right-wing Christians. Cultural disjuncture is becoming more expressive in town hall meetings across America, growing both in frequency and intensity. No one has fully connected the dots or completely understood the root of the anger, fear, and frustration, but at some point (and I believe it may be soon), prophetic voices will rise out of the mire, calling for a spiritual reboot in American culture. They will speak words that will ring truth, articulating for many what they feel but couldn't verbalize on their own. This will become a pivotal moment and will be the catalyst for reformation. The old order of things will begin to fade and the new will rise to take its place in history.

- **Priesthood of all believers**

The prophetic voices will likely not become the leaders of the revival, merely the voices that announce its arrival. Like in the days of Luther and Wesley, many of this generation will rise up knowing they are called with purpose. The work will expand not through the work of a few charismatic celebrities, but through the work of the "priesthood of all believers." Everyone will have a part to play, and because they will, the message of renewal will quickly spread and rapidly gain momentum.

* * *
In many ways, Millennials have seen biblical values being championed more by Democrats, who have been demonized by many conservative right-wing Christians.
* * *

Because Millennials will gravitate toward communities of truth, the work of the ministry will likely be an all hands-on deck event. Remembering that communities of truth are places where people want to sit in circles rather than in rows, where people discover truth rather than receiving it through lecture, and are places where everyone gets to play, leaders will likely take on very different job descriptions. They will be seen as facilitators, organizers, and trainers rather than Sunday pulpit preachers.

For those of us who have preached the gospel for most of our adult lives, we know something others may not. The truth is that the people who learn the most from any preaching or teaching are the teachers themselves. To succeed in the delivery of any message, a teacher eats, drinks, and sleeps the message, often putting in hours of study and preparation before any delivery. This process and experience should be shared. If it was, and I think it will be, leaders of the Re:Form will be far more grounded and passionate about the truths they profess.

- ## A new renaissance

Revisiting Luther's response to the Renaissance which accompanied the Reformation, a few important lessons should be learned and applied to a present-day awakening. Even though we are not presently breaking out of the dark ages, a few parallels still could be drawn. One major characteristic was how Catholicism, the established religious system of that day, reacted to science and enlightened thinking. Being extremely conservative, church leadership was threatened by new scientific evidence concerning how the natural world worked. They feared any new ideas and aggressively discredited them in fear of the common people looking other places for answers. Until that time, they had taken advantage of cultural illiteracy. By doing so, the priests became the sole interpreters of the written word, communicating its truths for the benefit of their own agendas. Luther, on the other hand, did the opposite. He took advantage of modern invention, the arts, and even science to affirm the truths he taught. He translated the Catholic Latin Bible into German and used Guttenberg's printing press to get a Bible into the hands of the people. He used art to provide visual imagery to support the Bible's many stories and ideas. Because Luther stimulated such a hunger to read the Bible on a personal level, the entire society advanced in literacy.

- ## Science and ingenuity

Religious conservatism in our day is guilty of these same mistakes. We, as Evangelicals, have had a track record of demonizing the scientific world. Many conservatives serve as the primary agency to push back on issues such as climate change for fear it will harm the Republican agenda. Creation vs. evolution has been a hill we have believed worthy of dying on rather than spending more energy on communicating the pure and simple gospel. Paul counseled Timothy to, "*Avoid foolish and ignorant debates*" (2 Timothy 2:23, NABRE), saying that they breed unnecessary quarrels. This was good advice, advice I think a new generation of Millennial Christians might follow better than we Baby Boomers did for so many years.

If there is to be Re:Form in the years ahead, I believe it will embrace renaissance as Luther did. There will be a new surge of creativity, and a convergence between the community of faith and innovation. Christians will become friends with the scientific community for the sake of ministering more effectively to a struggling world. In a quest to bring water to the thirsty and food to the hungry, young Christians will join arms with the scientific community to find solutions. God will give Christians supernatural insights to solve natural problems. Innovations will be found for carbon emission, renewable sources of energy, more efficient ways to grow organic, healthy food, and systems for water purification. Climatologists predict sea levels to rise three feet in this century as Antarctic ice begins to melt more rapidly than previously expected. This one simple fact will bring devastation to human kind. As Christian hearts turn with compassion toward suffering humanity, God will meet His people with new levels of creativity, giving Christianity favor in the world, rather than being perceived as a resisting force. Instead of being known as scoffers of prophesied end times' catastrophes, Christians will find themselves as servants working on the front lines of crisis.

- **The arts**

When we think of renaissance, we most often think of people like Leonardo di Vinci and Michelangelo. We think of sculpture, painting, the Sistine Chapel murals, and rightfully so, but there are many forms of the creative arts. There are new genres of music, poetry, and creative writing of every form. There are also new methods and forms of photography, videography, architecture, and amazingly innovative computer programs. With renaissance, the sky is not even the limit. Think of space exploration and the breathtaking new images satellites are sending from planets and solar systems thousands of light years away. We are in a new renaissance, and we may not fully be aware of it until we see it many years hence in historical retrospect. The church should be fully engaged in this handprint of the Lord, even as Luther was in his day. Even as he capitalized on the Guttenberg printing press and his use of lithographs to express the nature and heart of God to his world, the church in the near future will incorporate the use of cyberspace and artistic filmmaking in whole new creative ways to do the same. We will know when the Re:Form has come when we see the church embracing and aggressively engaging in art forms of every kind.

- ## The "New Song"

Again, reflecting back on revivals and spiritual awakenings from the past, we know new genres and styles of music have always emerged as fresh expressions of God's presence. It is hard to guess what the "new song" might sound like when the Millennials fully experience Re:Form, but the worship music accompanying their season of spiritual expression will be unique to them. It will minister to the culture of their generation as it has to past generations. Music will not only become a defining distinctive of the new movement, but will serve as a point of separation between Millennials and aging Evangelicals. Because music will minister more to one age group than another, frustrations will rise in many congregations who desire to serve multiple generations. In order for churches to cater to the demands of their people, churches will begin to provide several diverse music genres simultaneously during times of corporate congregational gatherings. In the end, however, the Millennials' style will dominate as uncomfortable Baby Boomers gravitate toward more traditional church settings.

- ## The rebirthing of the "Franciscan model of ministry" — a community of faith, meaning, and compassion

During the days of the Jesus Movement and other historical Christian movements, many young believers, both single and married, entered into communal lifestyles. During the '60s and '70s, a number of Christian communes were established along the California coast line. Close friends of mine, Steve and Layne Fish, led a commune they called the Lighthouse. They purchased an abandoned lighthouse on a jetty in the northern part of the state which housed over two hundred young people. It's hard to picture how a community made up of so many young people could operate without major problems, but they did. They lived in harmony, everyone having responsibilities and organized schedules to keep. They started

creative small businesses in the nearby towns as well as taking on refor-
estation projects for the National Forest Service to support their lifestyle.
They grew large gardens, raised small livestock and poultry, and attended
Bible studies and worship services throughout the week. While some of
the members from these communities ended up planting churches across
the country, others ended up in the developing world as missionaries. It
didn't last, but for a short time they did a lot of good.

In the early days of the Franciscan and Jesuit Catholic movements,
members all lived communal lifestyles. In their cases they were primarily
monks, but they too created sustainable missions that were powerfully
used to establish the Gospel throughout the world. They may have been
the most effective system of evangelism the world has known. Most all
of Mexico and Central and South America are Catholic to this day because of this creative model of ministry.

In the early 1700s, a friar named Father Junipero Serra, made a major
mark in what would later become California. Serra trained in Spain until
he was 35 years old, sailed to Mexico, and served the missions there for
twenty more years before walking from Mexico City, up the Baja penin-
sula, to what is now San Diego, California. Here, Serra established the
first of twenty-one mission bases that reached as far north as the city of
Monterey.

This is significant, because what Father Serra accomplished still
stands as an amazing model of compassion evangelism which is reproducible in today's world. Many can point to mistakes made by the early
Franciscans, largely due to their harsh theological perspective on the nature of God. Nevertheless, the fact remains that they did save thousands
of indigenous people from extreme oppression and trained them in skills,
lifting them out of severe poverty.

Father Serra started each base by building protective adobe walls fitted with gates that were only open in the light of day. This was to maintain
security and safety in a hostile land for those that committed themselves
to the Franciscan communal life. As California Indians came, the friars
trained them in new skills. They taught them to cultivate and farm the
land, to raise livestock, to construct buildings and shelters using the available natural resources, to weave, and to do woodworking. They made their
own furniture, vessels, musical instruments, and commodities of every

kind. The Franciscans showed the Indians how to filter water using rocks and charcoal and even established the first foundry in California. They educated the people, teaching them to speak the Spanish language, and to read. They provided medical help. They taught the Indians to sing and play the musical instruments they made. Each mission base became sustainable, not only producing its own food, but making wine from its many vineyards to sell to the Spanish who came to settle the land.

The Franciscan model was one that not only served the poor in practical ways, providing them with care and skill training, but brought them faith and hope. You might say, the Franciscans earned the right to share their faith because they served the people first with compassion.

* * *

You might say, the Franciscans earned the right to share their faith because they served the people first with compassion.

* * *

I say all this because I see it as a model for the future. The Franciscan model is a step beyond the Jesus Movement's model of communal living. I can see in the future, young people gaining professional skills useful in communal mission bases around the world, serving the poor. I see Millennials who have discovered God's good, perfect, and pleasing will for their lives. Young people who have discovered who they are in Christ and what He created them to do. I see them, after having been equipped for specific work, banning together in small, strategical groups, establishing Franciscan-type bases throughout the world, serving and demonstrating the love of God to the world. I see those trained as medics, midwifes, farmers, experts in animal husbandry, environmental skills, educators, construction and job-skill trainers, all uniting to serve communities and establish churches. I see this as a model that proved itself in the past and can be effectively adapted for a fresh, new work of God. This was, in part, what Paul spoke of in Romans 12. It is a model of reformation.

I see the cloud "rising"

Jesus said, "When you see a cloud rising in the west, you say, 'A rainstorm is coming', and it does." And then he said, "You hypocrites! You know how to interpret the appearance of the earth and the sky, but *how can you not know how **to interpret the present time?***' (Luke 12:54,56, NET).

It is time to see what's so clearly on the horizon. The cloud is rising and with it a people rising to become a powerful expression of God's love in a time when the culture is ripe and ready to receive it. The cloud is rising and though much of the present-day church will probably miss seeing it, some won't. God will take the remnant that are diligently looking and waiting and use them as His servants in a divine and amazing season of spiritual awakening. The culture is becoming ready, the cycles of history have given us previews of His coming attractions, and for those who are watchful of clouds, they can be assured an end of the age move of God is on the near horizon. As the cloud rises, so will those who God will use to lead the way.

Afterword

Living the Advent-ure

A number of years ago during a time when I desired a means to motivate my congregation to live a more radical Kingdom life, I taught a series called *"Living the Advent-ure."* I purposefully hyphenated the word adventure in an effort to create a play on the word. Living the advent-ure was defined as living a life of radical faith between the first and second "advent" of Jesus. Advent refers to the arrival or coming of Jesus, thus living the advent-ure speaks of a distinct way of living during a specific time period in human history. It is the time in which we now live. Jesus has come and is coming again. Jesus came revealing not only who He was as the Son of God, but He demonstrated to all humanity the heart of God. Jesus revealed that by receiving His free gift of grace, we humans could have intimate relationship with Him, not only now, but for eternity. He came and demonstrated the power of God's Kingdom and told us it was available not only later, after death, but now. As the Lord's Prayer professes, His Kingdom has come to earth as it is in heaven. It was ushered in by the work Jesus did for all humanity on the cross at Calvary.

Jesus not only provided us with a means of relationship with God, but commissioned those who received His gift, to participate with Him during this very unique period between His two advents. He told us to go into all the world and make disciples. He didn't tell us to live status quo lives, letting one day blend hopelessly into the next, waiting mindlessly for His second coming. No, He invited us to live the advent-ure; to live the greatest adventure life has to offer. He called us to live dangerously, not only discovering our divine purpose as He revealed to us in Romans 12, but to do it with zeal for the rest of our lives. He challenged us to take His message of love, forgiveness, and acceptance to every nook and cranny on the planet. To every people group, to the world's extreme poor, to the broken and hopeless, to the wealthy, to our neighbor, to every color, every nation, every generation. It's the greatest adventure, the greatest challenge, and the greatest privilege any human being could receive. It is an adventure of purpose and deep fulfillment. It is for anyone who would dare to accept and embrace who Jesus is, and then choose to live a radical life of faith. It's living the "Advent-ure".

Generations from the past have done it. The original disciples did it even unto death, and I believe when the Millennial generation discovers this truth, God will fill them with His Spirit to do it as well. I believe they will change their culture, change American culture, and impact the world they live in. Video games and mindless endeavors will lose their draw and they will refocus priorities, embrace Spiritual communities, and make lasting differences with their lives. They may well be the greatest advent-urers the world has ever known.

Check out a sample of Tri's timeless
leadership book, "Revolutionary Leadership."

Beginning a Revolution

Understanding the
Principles of Transformation

IMAGINE THE POSSIBILITIES of what can happen when God
begins to transform a community. It is infinite what God can do
when His people are both individually and corporately devoted to
following Him. For me, the endless possibilities started with a deflated helium balloon.

In the early spring of 1987, Michael Anderson was 12 years
old. He stood on the front lawn of his church in Ontario, Oregon,
holding a yellow, helium-filled balloon prepared earlier that morning in his Sunday School class. Inside the balloon, he had inserted
a scrap of notebook paper with the handwritten words, "Let us
love one another – 1 John 4:7 & 8." He released his balloon along
with the rest of the class. It slowly rose into the cold morning air,
drifting eastward with the prevailing wind toward the Idaho border.

A little over a year later in the summer of 1988, the last thing
on my mind was planting a church in Idaho. My wife, Nancy, and
I were happily situated in a growing Vineyard church in Southern
California. We felt secure and fulfilled in our ministry as associate
pastors at the Desert Vineyard Christian Fellowship in Lancaster,
California.

Nancy and I fell in love 20 years earlier when we met as students at the College of Idaho (now Albertson College) in Caldwell,
Idaho. We married in 1970 and remained in Caldwell as newlyweds

for two more years before moving to the mountains of California to raise our children on my family's ranch. I went to work as a schoolteacher for several years before joining the church staff in Lancaster.

In 1988, we received a phone call from an old Idaho friend. Pat Armstrong, who had remained close with me and Nancy since our college days, made his living building backcountry trails with a team of mules. We had often spent several of our summer breaks working for Pat while I was still teaching school.

At the time I received Pat's phone call, we hadn't worked for him in several years due to our responsibilities at the church. However, he called to ask for help on a project to reconstruct a damaged airstrip on the Middle Fork of the Salmon River. With a couple of weeks of vacation, we jumped at the opportunity and headed 800 miles north to Idaho. Our kids, Kate and Brook, had heard many stories about our early days in Idaho but had never visited the state themselves. We were all content with our lifestyle on the family ranch. None of us had even considered leaving our comfortable California lifestyle – that is, until we passed through Boise on our way to meet Pat.

Vision never announces its coming, but when it comes, you know it. And before I knew it, vision was on my front porch, knocking loudly on the door.

I can't explain what happened that day, but I believe it was supernatural – our whole family fell in love with the city. God was definitely doing something in all of our hearts, but I was the last to admit it. Privately, Nancy asked me if I would ever consider giving up our life in California to plant a Vineyard church in Boise. Suddenly, fear began to stir in me because I had witnessed so many church plant failures. Without much thought, I defiantly answered, "No!" And I informed her that I didn't want to talk about it again.

Two days later, we flew into Pat's camp on Mahoney Creek. Everyone was enjoying the time in the wilderness, except me. I was miserable. For many years, I had waited to get back to the mountains of Idaho, but I was not enjoying it. The thought of leaving the security of my established life really bothered me. Leaving the ranch, risking everything, transplanting our family to an unknown place with no friends – it all seemed totally crazy and impractical.

Noticing my struggle, Nancy suggested that I take a long walk and get alone with God. Because of my attitude, I perceived her as really saying, "Why don't you take a hike?" Climbing a tall mountain adjacent to Mahoney Creek, I only stopped to catch my breath and pray. At one point, I remember crying out to God for an answer.

"Lord," I said, "I desperately need a word from you." But every time I stopped hiking, I never heard His voice. Then I figured God would speak to me once I made it to the summit, just as He spoke to Moses on Mt. Sinai. But His voice was absolutely quiet. Finally, I decided to stop guessing how God would speak to me and just enjoy the time I had in the backcountry with my family and friends.

As I began walking down an aspen-covered ridge, something caught my eye on the opposite side of the ravine. The bright yellow object looked out of place for the colors on the mountain terrain. Intrigued by this object, I ventured closer to see what it was.

I descended the ravine and scrambled up the opposite side. After climbing under a thorny berry bush, I emerged carrying Michael Anderson's deflated yellow balloon with an illustration of Noah's ark printed on the side. I sensed this particular balloon had been sent to me from the Lord and that it contained a message in it from Him. I felt the balloon and there was a small note inside. At first, I was almost afraid to remove it. I climbed back up the side of the ravine to a bright sunny spot and sat down. I ripped a small hole on the side of the balloon to remove the paper.

Here I was, sitting on a mountainside in the very center of the largest wilderness area in the continental United States. I had prayed all day for a word from God. As you can guess, the note read, "Let us love one another – 1 John 4:7 & 8." Oddly enough, at the time I remember telling the Lord that I needed a real word, a more specific answer to my question.

It was then that the Lord spoke to me through the Holy Spirit more clearly than I had ever heard Him before. He said, "Tri, I don't care where you do it. All I want you to do is build a church that loves people." Then He asked me, "Do you want to do it in Boise, Idaho?" It was at that moment that I discovered what He had already put in my heart. Without hesitating, I replied, "Yes, Lord, I do."

Later that morning, I wandered back into our camp at Mahoney Creek and found Nancy by the fire. She asked me if I had heard anything from the Lord. I pulled the balloon and small strip of notebook paper from my pocket, telling her that God had written me a note.

What God was giving me was a vision I couldn't accomplish on my own or even with just my family. I needed several others to journey with me and make this vision from God a reality in the city of Boise. It was almost one year to the day from finding the balloon that we found ourselves back in Boise with 13 other families from the Lancaster church. They, too, felt God's call to go plant a church in Boise that would love people. This team of people would have not been able to fulfill this vision had they gone out alone. But together, we were a collection of believers who trusted that God was going to help us accomplish the purpose He had set before us.

Today, Michael Anderson's balloon is framed on my office wall. I often look at that note and remember God's faithfulness and His very clear commission for us to build a church where people love one another.

* * *

To keep reading, purchase REVOLUTIONARY LEADERSHIP online at Amazon.com or where other fine books are sold.

Made in the USA
Middletown, DE
30 March 2018